D0983396

AMERICAN EDUCATION

Its Men

Ideas

and

Institutions

The District School As It Was

Warren Burton

ARNO PRESS & THE NEW YORK TIMES
New York * *1969*

Reprint edition 1969 by Arno Press, Inc.

*

Library of Congress Catalog Card No. 71-89157

*

Reprinted from a copy in Teachers College Library

*

Manufactured in the United States of America

Editorial Note

AMERICAN EDUCATION: *Its Men, Institutions and Ideas* presents selected works of thought and scholarship that have long been out of print or otherwise unavailable. Inevitably, such works will include particular ideas and doctrines that have been outmoded or superseded by more recent research. Nevertheless, all retain their place in the literature, having influenced educational thought and practice in their own time and having provided the basis for subsequent scholarship.

Lawrence A. Cremin
Teachers College

The District School
As It Was

THE
DISTRICT SCHOOL
AS IT WAS

BY ONE WHO
WENT TO IT

EDITED BY

CLIFTON JOHNSON

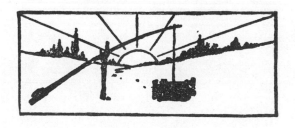

T. Y. CROWELL COMPANY
NEW YORK

Contents

Introduction

THE New England schools of the early part of the last century had a primitive picturesqueness that makes them seem of a much more remote past than they really are. The wood-pile in the yard, the open fire-place, the backless benches on which the smaller scholars sat, and the two terms — one in winter under a master, and one in summer ruled by a mistress — have the flavor of pioneer days. In this seeming remoteness, coupled with its actual nearness, lies the chief reason for the charm that this period has for us. The intervening hundred or more years have destroyed every vestige of the old school sights and customs. We have only fragmentary reminiscences left. But the more the facts fade, the more they allure us. We are bringing the old furniture down from the garrets, and setting it forth in the places of honor in our best rooms; and the

same feeling that prompts this love for an ancient chair or "chest of drawers" makes us
prize the reminiscences of bygone times as age
gives them an increasing rarity.

Here, then, is "The District School As It
Was." I know of no brighter, more graphic
impressions of the school-days of the first quarter
of the nineteenth century. The descriptions
have an unusual degree of simplicity and charm,
and at the same time are spiced with a sparkle
of humor that makes them good reading, apart
from any historic attraction.

The book was first published in Boston, in
1833, where it was received "with unqualified
favor." A little later it was brought out in
New York, with equal success, and a few years
afterward a London edition was issued as giving
a faithful description of one of the institutions
of New England.

In 1852 "The District School," with several
lesser works by the same writer, was published
in a twelvemo volume of 364 pages, "to be disposed of to subscribers for the benefit of the
Author." The longest of the additional writings had been previously published as a separate
book entitled "The Scenery Shower." But it
was found that to the mystified mind of the
average reader this title was understood to mean

"The Scenery Rainfall," and a change was made in the reissue to "Scenery Showing." Aside from "The District School" and the ingenious "Supplication to the People of the United States," which makes a supplementary chapter in the present volume, the author's works in the 1852 book are mild, contemplative essays of no particular value.   The idea of the "Supplication," just referred to, is so odd and the list of mispronounced words is so characteristic of the country folk of fifty or seventy-five years ago, that it is well worth preserving. , These words can be heard even now among the old people of out-of-the-way villages, and they repeat them with the same nasal twang that was familiar to the ears of our grandparents.

The author of "The District School," Rev. Warren Burton, was born in Wilton, N. H., in 1800, and died at Salem, Mass., in 1866.   The school he describes is the one he himself went to as a youth in his native town.   His attendance began at the age of three-and-one-half in the summer of 1804 and ended with the winter term of 1817–1818, when he had arrived at the dignity of being one of the big boys on the back seat. Sixteen years later his book was published, describing the school "as it was," and the reader is given to understand that the shortcomings he

pictured were no longer characteristic, so far as
New England was concerned. It gives an odd
impression to see the school viewed across this
narrow space, as if in contrast with the enlight-
enment of 1833 and the improvements by then
accomplished, the teaching methods and school
environment of the earlier period were a part
of the dark ages.

After he left the district school Mr. Burton
prepared himself for Harvard College, where he
graduated in 1821. Then followed several
years of teaching. Next we find him taking
the Harvard Theological Course, and in 1828
he was ordained as a Unitarian minister at East
Cambridge. As a preacher he served in Washington, Keene and Nashua in New Hampshire,
and in Hingham, Waltham, Worcester, and
Boston in Massachusetts. But as time went
on he preached less and devoted himself more
and more to objects of reform. He was a frequent contributor to periodicals, and in both
writing and lecturing he labored to promote
home culture and to improve the conditions of
the schools. Friends speak of him as being
rather tall, with a most benevolent countenance
and gentle manners. His published works include several volumes on religion and education,
and, in lighter vein, these recollections of his

school-days and a little book printed anonymously entitled " The Village Choir " — a humorous description of the ways and manners, quarrels and jealousies of an old-time choir in a country church.

The text in the present edition of " The District School " is practically what it was in the original. Nothing is changed, and the editing consists in a slight condensation, effected by cutting out unnecessary asides and digressions.

With the exception of a few special drawings, the illustrations are cuts from old spellers and other books of the period. I have a number of these books before me as I write. The arithmetics, grammars, and readers are sober volumes bound in full sheep. The stiff bindings are warped and battered now, the pages yellow and spotty, and they have a musty odor of age and of long years spent in dusty garret corners.

The old spellers are not much gayer. They have thin sides of light, splintery wood pasted over with dull gray paper. But inside there is a good deal of variety, — words from one syllable up to ponderous sixes, wise maxims, religious instruction, and many little stories with never-failing morals under their sugar coats. Lastly, there is a sprinkling of curious pictures. Both pictures and text have an unconscious humor that would put a professional wit to shame. No one by forethought could make more quaint distortions of fact and human nature. It gives the same feeling as if one were looking out on the world through the flaws of an old-time window-pane.

In the body of the book are various fac-simile reproductions from the old spellers; but in closing my introduction I would like to re-print a few more bits here. For instance, take this, which is from a speller lesson for beginners.

Pigs can dig in the side of a hill.
A pig drinks swill.
Let him drink his fill of swill and milk.

The lesson following the above is this : —

Ships sail on the sea.
A ship will hold ten nags, ten hens, for-ty cats and pigs, six beds, six-ty men, and much more.

A dozen pages farther on we come to some-thing more serious — the " Story of a Bad Boy."

Jack lov-ed to play more than he lov-ed to go to school. So he stop-ped by the way to slide on a pond. He had not slid long when he slipt into a hole cut in the ice. There he was left to hang by his hands on the cold ice, and his feet and legs in the cold water. O how sor-ry that he ran a-way from school! How glad and yet how sha-med, when his pa came and took him home in his arms!

Then here is a lesson designed to teach the child in an agreeable way something of natural history.

OF SHEEP, HORSES, AND BIRDS.

What has Charles got to keep him warm?

Charles has got a frock and warm petticoats.

And what have the poor sheep got; have they petticoats?

The sheep have got wool, thick, warm wool. Feel it. Oh, it is very comfortable! That is their clothing.

And what have horses got?

Horses have got long hair; and cows have hair.

And what have pigs got?

Pigs have got bristles and hair.

And what have birds got?

Birds have got feathers; soft, clean, shining feathers.

Birds build nests in trees; that is their house.

Can you climb a tree?

No.   I am afraid I should fall and break my bones.

Ask puss to teach you; she can climb.   See how fast she climbs!   She is at the top.   She wants to catch birds.   Pray, puss, do not take the little birds that sing so merrily!   She has got a sparrow in her mouth.   She has eaten it all up.   No, here are two or three feathers on the ground, all bloody.   Poor sparrow!

Finally, here are a few sentences from the latter part of the spellers, apparently put in to fill a blank space at the bottom of a page.

A wise child will not learn to chew tobacco, smoke the pipe, or cigars, or take snuff, for the four following reasons : —

They are *dirty* habits; *useless* habits; *costly* habits; *slavish* habits.   It is pitiful to see a strong, healthy looking man a slave to a quid of tobacco, or a puff of smoke; or a beautiful, sensible lady stuffed up or bedaubed with snuff.

CLIFTON JOHNSON.

HADLEY, MASS.

The District School As It Was

Chapter I

The Old School-house

THE Old School-house, how distinctly it rises to existence anew before the eye of my mind! It is now no more; and those of similar construction are passing away, never to be patterned again. It may be well, therefore, to describe the edifice wherein and whereabout occurred many of the scenes about to be recorded. I would have future generations acquainted with the accommodations, or rather dis-accommodations, of their predecessors.

The Old School-house, in District No. 5, stood on the top of a very high hill, on the north side of what was called the County road. The house of Capt. Clark, about ten rods off, was the only human dwelling within a quarter of a mile. The reason why this seminary of letters was perched so high in the air, and so far from the homes of those who resorted to it, was this : — Here was the center of the district, as near as surveyor's chain could designate. The people east would not permit the building to be carried one rod further west, and those of the opposite quarter were as obstinate on their side.

The edifice was set half in Capt. Clark's field, and half in the road. The wood-pile lay in the corner made by the east end and the stone wall. The best roof it ever had over it was the changeful sky, which was a little too leaky to keep the fuel at all times fit for combustion, without a great deal of puffing and smoke. The doorstep was a broad unhewn rock, brought from the neighboring pasture. It had not a flat and even surface, but was considerably sloping from the door to the road ; so that, in icy times, the scholars, in passing out, used to snatch from the scant declivity the transitory pleasure of a slide. But look out for a slip-up, ye careless ; for many a time have I seen an urchin's head where his feet were but a second before. And once, the most lofty and perpendicular pedagogue I ever knew, became suddenly horizontalized in his egress.

But we have lingered round this door-step long enough. Before we cross it, however, let us just glance at the outer side of the structure.

It was never painted by man; but the clouds of many years had stained it with their own dark hue. The nails were starting from their fastness, and fellow-clapboards were becoming less closely and warmly intimate. There were six windows, which here and there stopped and distorted the passage of light by fractures, patches, and seams of putty. There were shutters of board, like those of a store, which were of no kind of use, excepting to keep the windows from harm in vacations, when they were the least liable to harm. They might have been convenient screens against the summer sun, were it not that their shade was inconvenient darkness. Some of these, from loss of buttons, were fastened back by poles, which were occasionally thrown down in the heedlessness of play, and not replaced till repeated slams had broken a pane of glass, or the patience of the teacher. To crown this description of externals, I must say a word about the roof. The shingles had been battered apart by a thousand rains; and, excepting where the most defective had been exchanged for new ones, they were dingy with the mold and moss of time. The bricks of the chimney-top were losing their cement, and looked as if some high wind might hurl them from their smoky vocation.

We will now go inside. First, there is an entry which the district were sometimes provident enough to store with dry pine wood, as an antagonist to the greenness and wetness of the other fuel. A door on the left admits us to the school-room. Here is a space about twenty feet long and ten wide, the reading and spelling parade. At the south end of it, at the left as you enter, was one seat and writing bench, making a right angle with the rest of the seats. This was occupied in the winter by two of the oldest males in the school. At the opposite end was the magisterial desk, raised upon a platform a foot from the floor. The fire-place was on the right, half way between the door of entrance and another door leading into a dark closet, where the girls put their outside garments and their dinner baskets. This also served as a fearful dungeon for the immuring of offenders. Directly opposite the fire-place was an aisle, two feet and a half wide, running up an inclined floor to the opposite side of the room. On each side of this were five or six long seats and writing benches, for the accommodation of the school at their studies. In front of these, next to the spelling floor, were low, narrow seats for abecedarians and others near that rank. In general, the older the scholar, the further from the front was his location. The windows behind the back seat were so low that the traveler could generally catch the stealthy glance of curiosity as he passed. Such was the Old School-house at the time I first entered it. Its subsequent condition and many other inconveniences will be noticed hereafter.

Chapter II

First Summer at School — Mary Smith

I WAS three years and a half old when I first entered the Old School-house as an abecedarian. I ought, perhaps, to have set foot on the first step of learning's ladder before this; but I had no elder brother or sister to lead me to school, a mile off; and it never occurred to my good parents, that they could teach me even the alphabet; or, perhaps, they could not afford the time, or muster the patience for the tedious process. I had, however, learned the name of capital A, because it stood at the head of the column, and was the similitude of a harrow frame; of O, also, from its resemblance to a hoop. Its sonorous name, moreover, was a frequent passenger through my mouth, after I had begun to articulate; its ample sound being the most natural medium by which man, born unto trouble, signifies the pains of his lot. X, too, was familiar, as it seemed so like the end of the old saw-horse that stood in the woodshed. Further than this my alphabetical lore did not extend, according to present recollection.

I shall never forget my first day of scholarship, as it was the most important era which had yet occurred to my experience. Behold me on the eventful morning of the first Monday in June, arrayed in my new jacket and trowsers, into which my importance had been shoved for the first time in my life. This change in my costume had been deferred till this day, that I might be " all nice and clean to go to school." Then my Sunday hat of coarse and hard sheep's wool adorned my head for the first time in common week-day use; for my other had been crushed, torn, and soiled out of the seemliness, and almost out of the form, of a hat. My little new basket, too, bought expressly for the purpose, was laden with 'lection-cake and cheese for my dinner, and slung upon my arm. An old Perry's spelling-book, that our boy Ben used at the winter school, completed my equipment.

Mary Smith was my first teacher, and the dearest to my heart I ever had. She was a niece of Mrs. Carter, who lived in the nearest house on the way to school. She had visited her aunt the winter before; and her uncle, being chosen committee for the school at the town-meeting in the spring, sent immediately to her home in Connecticut, and engaged her to teach the summer school. During the few days she spent at his house, she had shown herself peculiarly qualified to interest, and to gain the love of children. Some of the neighbors, too, who had dropped in while she was there, were much pleased with her appearance. She had taught one season in her native State; and that she succeeded well, Mr. Carter could not doubt. He preferred her, therefore, to hundreds near by; and for once the partiality of the relative proved profitable to the district.

Now Mary Smith was to board at her uncle's. This was deemed a fortunate circumstance on my account, as she would take care of me on the way, which was needful to my inexperienced childhood.

She used to lead me to school by the hand, while John and Sarah Carter gamboled on, unless I chose to gambol with them; but the first day, at least, I kept by her side. All her demeanor toward me, and indeed toward us all, was of a piece with her first introduction. She called me to her to read, not with a look and voice as if she were doing a duty she disliked, and was determined I should do mine too, like it or not, as is often the manner of teachers;

but with a cheerful smile, as if she were at a pastime.

My first business was to master the A B C, and no small achievement it was; for many a little learner waddles to school through the summer, and wallows to the same through the winter, before he accomplishes it, if he happens to be taught in the manner of former times. This might have been my lot, had it not been for Mary Smith. Few of the better methods of teaching, which now make the road to knowledge so much more easy and pleasant, had then found their way out of, or into, the brain of the pedagogical vocation. Mary went on in the old way indeed; but the whole exercise was done with such sweetness on her part, that the dilatory and usually unpleasant task was to me a pleasure, and by the close of that summer, the alphabet was securely my own.

That hardest of all tasks, sitting becomingly still, was rendered easier by her goodness. When I grew restless, and turned from side to side, and changed from posture to posture, in search of relief from my uncomfortableness, she spoke words of sympathy rather than reproof. Thus I was won to be as quiet as I could. When I grew drowsy, and needed but a comfortable position to drop into sleep and forget-

fulness of the weary hours, she would gently
lay me at length on my seat, and leave me just
falling to slumber, with her sweet smile the last
thing beheld or remembered.

Thus wore away my first summer at the
district school. As I look back on it, faintly
traced on memory, it seems like a beautiful
dream, the images of which are all softness
and peace. I recollect that, when the last day
came, it was not one of light-hearted joy — it
was one of sadness, and it closed in tears. I
was now obliged to stay at home in solitude,
for the want of playmates, and in weariness of
the passing time, for the want of something
to do; as there was no particular pleasure in
saying A B C all alone, with no Mary Smith's
voice and looks for an accompaniment.

Chapter III

The Spelling-book

AS the spelling-book was the first manual of instruction used in school, and kept in our hands for many years, I think it worthy of a separate chapter in these annals of the times that are past. The spelling-book used in our school from time immemorial — immemorial at least to the generation of learners to which I belonged — was thus entitled: "THE ONLY SURE GUIDE to the English Tongue, by William Perry, Lecturer of the English Language in the Academy of Edinburgh, and author of several valuable school-books."

In the first place, there was a frontispiece. This frontispiece consisted of two parts. In the upper division, there was the representation of a tree laden with fruit of the largest description. It was intended, I presume, as a striking and alluring emblem of the general subject, the particular branches, and the rich fruits of education. But the figurative meaning was above my apprehension, and no one took the trouble to explain it. I supposed it nothing but the picture of a luxuriant apple-tree; and it always made me think of that good tree in my father's orchard, so dear to my palate, — the pumpkin-sweeting.

There ran a ladder from the ground up among the branches, which was designed to represent the ladder of learning. Little boys were ascending this in pursuit of the fruit that hung there so temptingly. Others were already up in the tree, plucking the apples directly from their stems; while others were on the ground, picking up those that had dropped in their ripeness. At the very top of the tree, with his head reared above all fruit or foliage, was a bare-headed lad with a book in his hand, which he seemed intently studying. I supposed that he was a boy that loved his book better than apples, as all good boys should, — one who in very childhood had trodden temptation under foot. But, indeed, it was only a boy who was gathering fruit from the topmost boughs, according to the figurative meaning, as the others were from those lower down. Or rather, as he was portrayed, he seemed like one who had culled the fairest and highest growing apples, and was trying to learn from a book where he should find a fresh and loftier tree, upon which he might climb to a richer repast and a nobler distinction.

This picture used to retain my eye longer than any other in the book. It was probably more agreeable on account of the other part of the frontispiece below it. This was the representation of a school at their studies, with the master at his desk. He was pictured as an elderly man, with an immense wig enveloping his head and bagging about his neck, and with a face that had an expression of perplexity at a sentence in parsing, or a sum in arithmetic, and a frown at the playful urchins in the distant seats. There could not have been a more capital device by which the pleasures of a free range and delicious eating, both so dear to the young, might be contrasted with stupefying confinement and longing palates in the presence of crabbed authority. The subsequent contents I was going on to describe in detail; but on second thought I forbear, for fear that the description might be as tedious to my readers as the study of them was to me. Suffice it to say, there was talk about vowels and consonants, diphthongs and triphthongs, monosyllables and polysyllables, orthography and punctuation, and even about geography, all which was about as intelligible to us, who were obliged to commit it to memory year after year, as the fee-faw-fum uttered by the giant in one of our story-books.

Perry's spelling-book, as it was in those days, at least, is now out of use. It is nowhere to be found except in fragments in some dark corner of a country cupboard or garret. All vestiges of it will soon disappear forever. What will the rising generations do, into what wilds of barbarism will they wander, into what pits of ignorance fall, without the aid of the Only Sure Guide to the English tongue?

Chapter IV

First Winter at School

HOW I longed for the winter school to begin, to which I looked forward as a relief from my do-nothing days, and as a renewal, in part at least, of the soft and glowing pleasures of the past summer! But the schoolmaster, the thought of him was a fearful looking-for of frowns and ferulings. Had I not heard our Ben tell of the direful punishments of the winter school; of the tingling hand, black and blue with twenty strokes, and not to be closed for a fortnight from soreness? Did not the minister and the schoolmaster of the preceding winter visit together at our house, one evening, and did I not think the schoolmaster far the more awful man of the two? The minister took me in his lap, gave me a kiss, and told me about his own little Charley at home, whom I must come to see; and he set me down with the impression that he was not half so terrible as I had thought him. But the schoolmaster condescended to no words with

me. He was as stiff and unstooping as the
long kitchen fire-shovel, and as solemn of face
as a cloudy fast-day.

The winter at length came, and the first day
of the school was fixed and made known, and
the longed-for morning finally arrived. With
hoping, yet fearing heart, I was led by Ben to
school. But my fears respecting the teacher
were not realized that winter. He had nothing particularly remarkable about him to my
little mind. He had his hands too full of the
great things of the great scholars to take much
notice of me, excepting to hear me read my
Abs four times a day. This exercise he went
through like a great machine, and I like a little
one; so monotonous was the humdrum and
regular the recurrence of *ab*, *eb*, *ib*, *ob*, *ub*, &c.,
from day to day, and week to week. To recur
to the metaphor of a ladder by which progress
in learning is so often illustrated, I was all
summer on the lowest round, as it were, lifting
first one foot and then the other, still putting it
down in the same place, without going any
higher; and all winter, while at school, I was
as wearily tap-tapping it on the second step.

There was one circumstance, however, in
the daily routine, which was a matter of some
little excitement and pleasure. I was put into

a class. Truly my littleness, feelingly, if not
actually and visibly, enlarged itself, when I was
called out with Sam Allen, Henry Green, and
Susan Clark, to take our stand on the floor as
the sixth class. I marched up with the tread
of a soldier; and, thinks I, " Who has a better
right to be at the head than myself ? " so the
head I took, as stiff and as straight as a cob.
My voice, too, if it lost none of its treble, was
pitched a key louder, as *a—b ab* rang through
the realm. And when we had finished, I
looked up among the large scholars, as I strutted
to my seat, with the thought, " I am almost as
big as you now," puffing out my tiny soul.
Now, moreover, I held the book in my own
hand, and kept the place with my own finger,
instead of standing like a very little boy, with
my hands at my side, following with my eye
the point of the mistress's scissors.

There was one terror at this winter school
which I must not omit in this chronicle of my
childhood. It arose from the circumstance of
meeting so many faces which I had never seen
before, or at least had never seen crowded
together in one body. All the great boys and
girls, who had been kept at home during the
summer, now left axes and shovels, needles and
spinning wheels, and poured into the winter

c

school.   There they sat, side by side, head after
head, row above row.   For this I did not care ;
but every time the master spoke to me for any
little misdemeanor, it seemed as if all turned
their eyes on my timid self, and I felt petrified
by the gaze.   But this simultaneous and con-
centrated eye-shot was the most distressing
when I happened late, and was obliged to go in
after the school were all seated in front of my
advance.

The severest duty I was ever called to perform was sitting on that little front seat, at my
first winter school.   My lesson in the Abs conveyed no ideas, excited no interest, and, of
course, occupied but very little of my time.
There was nothing before me on which to lean
my head, or lay my arms, but my own knees.
I could not lie down to drowse, as in summer,
for want of room on the crowded seat.   How
my limbs ached for the freedom and activity of
play !   It sometimes seemed as if a drubbing
from the master, or a kick across the school-
house, would have been a pleasant relief.

But these bonds upon my limbs were not all.
I had trials by fire in addition.   Every cold
forenoon, the old fire-place, wide and deep, was
kept a roaring furnace of flame, for the benefit
of blue noses, chattering jaws, and aching toes,

in the more distant regions. The end of my seat, just opposite the chimney, was oozy with melted pitch, and sometimes almost smoked with combustion. Judge, then, of what living flesh had to bear. It was a toil to exist. I truly ate the bread of instruction, or rather nibbled at the crust of it, in the sweat of my face.

But the pleasures and the pains of this season at school did not continue long. After a few weeks, the storms and drifts of midwinter kept me mostly at home. Henry Allen was in the same predicament. As for Susan Clark, she did not go at all after the first three or four days. In consequence of the sudden change from roasting within doors to freezing without, she took a violent cold, and was sick all winter.

Chapter V

Second Summer — Mary Smith Again

THE next summer, Mary Smith was the mistress again. She gave such admirable satisfaction, that there was but one unanimous wish
that she should be re-engaged. Unanimous, I
said, but it was not quite so; for Capt. Clark,
who lived close by the school-house, preferred
somebody else, no matter whom, fit or not fit,
who should board with him, as the teachers
usually did. But Mary would board with her
Aunt Carter, as before. Then Mr. Patch's
family grumbled not a little, and tried to find
fault; for they wanted their Polly should keep
the school and board at home, and help her
mother night and morning, and save the pay
for the board to boot. Otherwise Polly must
go into a distant district, to less advantage to
the family purse. Mrs. Patch was heard to
guess that " Polly could keep as good a school
as anybody else. Her education had cost
enough anyhow. She had been to our school
summer after summer, and winter after winter,

ever since she was a little gal, and had then
been to the 'cademy three months besides. She
had moreover taught three summers already,
and was twenty-one; whereas Mary Smith had
taught but two, and was only nineteen." But
the committee had not such confidence in the
experienced Polly's qualifications. All who had
been to school with her knew that her head
was dough, if ever head was. And all who
had observed her school-keeping career (she
never kept but once in the same place) pretty
soon came to the same conclusion, notwithstanding her loaf of brains had been three
months in that intellectual oven called by her
mother the 'cademy.

So Mary Smith kept the school, and I had
another delightful summer under her care and
instruction. I was four years and a half old
now, and had grown an inch. I was no tiny,
whining, half-scared baby, as in the first summer. No, indeed; I had been to the winter
school, had read in a class, and had stood up
at the fire with the great boys, had seen a
snow-ball fight, and had been accidentally hit
once by the icy missile of big-fisted Joe Swagger.

I looked down upon two or three fresh, slob-
bering abecedarians with a pride of superiority,
greater perhaps than I ever felt again. We

read not in *ab*, *eb*, &c., but in words that meant
something; and, before the close of the summer, in what were called the "Reading Lessons," that is, little words arranged in little
sentences.

Mary was the same sweet angel this season
as the last. She was forced to caution us
younglings pretty often; yet a caution from
her was as effectual as would be a frown, and
indeed a blow, from many others. At least, so
it was with me. She used to resort to various
severities with the refractory and idle, and in
one instance she used the ferule; but we all
knew, and the culprit knew, that it was well
deserved.

At the close of the school, there was a deeper
sadness in our hearts than on the last summer's
closing day. She had told us that she should
never be our teacher again, — should probably
never meet many of us again in this world.
She gave us much parting advice about loving
and obeying God, and loving and doing good
to everybody. She shed tears as she talked to
us, and when we were dismissed, the customary
and giddy laugh was not heard. Many were
sobbing with grief, and even the least sensitive
were softened and subdued to an unusual quiet-
ness.

The last time I ever saw Mary was Sunday evening, on my way home from meeting. As we passed Mr. Carter's, she came out to the chaise where I sat between my parents, to bid us good-by. The next morning she left for her native town; and before another summer, she was married. As Mr. Carter soon moved from our neighborhood, the dear instructress never visited it again.

Chapter VI

Third Summer — Mehitabel Holt and Other Instructresses

THIS summer, a person named Mehitabel Holt was our teacher. It was with eager delight that I set out for school on the first morning. I longed for the companionship and the sports of school. I had heard nothing about the mistress, excepting that she was an experienced and approved one. On my way, the image of something like Mary Smith arose to my imagination; a young lady with pleasant face and voice, and a winning gentleness of manner. This was natural; for Mary was the only mistress I had ever been to, and in fact the only one I had ever seen, who made any impression on my mind in her school-keeping capacity. What, then, was my surprise when my eyes first fell on Mehitabel Holt! I shall not describe how nature had made her, or time had altered her. She had been well-looking, indeed rather beautiful once, I have heard; but, if so, the acidity of her temper had diffused itself through, and lamentably corroded this valued gift of nature.

She kept order; for her punishments were horrible, especially to us little ones. She dungeoned us in that windowless closet just for a whisper. She tied us to her chair-post for an hour, because sportive nature tempted our fingers and toes into something like play. If we were restless on our seats, wearied of our posture, fretted by the heat, or sick of the unintelligible lesson, a twist of the ear, or a snap on the head from her thimbled finger, reminded us that sitting perfectly still was the most important virtue of a little boy in school. Our forenoon and afternoon recess was allowed to be five minutes only; and, even during that time, our voices must not rise above the tone of quiet conversation. That delightful exercise of juvenile lungs, hallooing, was a capital crime. Our noonings, in which we used formerly to rejoice in the utmost freedom of legs and lungs, were now like the noonings of the Sabbath, in the restraints imposed upon us. As Mehitabel boarded at Capt. Clark's, any ranging in the fields, or raising of the voice, was easily detected by her watchful senses.

As the prevalent idea in those days respecting a good school was, that there should be no more

sound and motion than was absolutely necessary, Mehitabel was, on the whole, popular with
the parents. She kept us still, and forced us to
get our lessons; and that was something uncommon in a mistress. So she was employed
the next summer to keep our childhood in
bondage. Had her strict rules been enforced
by anything resembling Mary Smith's sweet
and sympathetic disposition and manners, they
would have been endurable. But, as it was,
our schooling those two summers was a pain
to the body, a weariness to the mind, and a
disgust to the heart.

I shall not devote a separate chapter to all
my summer teachers. What more I may have
to say of them I shall put into this. They
were none of them like Mehitabel in severity,
nor all of them equal to her in usefulness, and
none of them equal in any respect to Mary
Smith. Some were very young, scarcely sixteen, and as unfit to manage that " harp of a
thousand strings," the human mind, as is the
unskilled and changeful wind to manage any
musical instrument by which science and taste
delight the ear. Some kept tolerable order;
others made the attempt, but did not succeed;
others did not even make the attempt. All
would doubtless have done better, had they

been properly educated and disciplined themselves.

After I was ten years old, I ceased to attend the summer school except in foul weather, as in fair I was wanted at home on the farm. These scattering days, I and others of nearly the same age were sent to school by our parents, in hopes that we should get at least a snatch of knowledge. But this rainy-day schooling was nothing but vanity to us, and vexation of spirit to the mistress. We could read and spell better than the younger and regular scholars, and were puffed up with our own superiority. We showed our contempt for the mistress and her orders, by doing mischief ourselves, and leading others into temptation.

If she had the boldness to apply the ferule, we laughed in her face, unless her blows were laid on with something like masculine strength. In case of such severity, we waited for our revenge till the close of the school for the day, when we took the liberty to let saucy words reach her ear, especially if the next day was likely to be fair, and we of course were not to re-appear in her realm till foul weather again.

Chapter VII

Little Books presented the Last Day of the School

THERE was one circumstance connected with the history of summer schools of so great importance to little folks, that it must not be omitted. It was this. The mistress felt obliged to give little books to all her pupils on the closing day of her school. Otherwise she would be thought stingy, and half the good she had done during the summer would be canceled by the omission of the expected donations. If she had the least generosity, or hoped to be remembered with any respect and affection, she must devote a week's wages, and perhaps more, to the purchase of these little toy-books. My first present, of course, was from Mary Smith. It was not a little book the first summer, but it was something that pleased me more.

The last day of the school had arrived. All were sad that it was now to finish. My only solace was that I should now have a little book, for I was not unmoved in the general expectation that prevailed. After the reading and spelling, and all the usual exercises of the school, were over, Mary took from her desk a pile of the glittering little things we were looking for. What beautiful covers, — red, yellow, blue, green! All eyes were now centered on the outspread treasures. Admiration and expectation were depicted on every face. Pleasure glowed in every heart; for the worst, as well as the best, calculated with certainty on a present. The scholars were called out one by one to receive the dazzling gifts, beginning at the oldest. I, being an abecedarian, must wait till the last; but as I knew that my turn would surely come in due order, I was tolerably patient. But what was my disappointment, my exceeding bitterness of grief, when the last book on Mary's lap was given away, and my name not yet called! Every one present had received, except myself and two others of the A B C rank. I felt the tears starting to my eyes; my lips were drawn to their closest pucker to hold in my emotions from audible outcry. I heard my fellow-sufferer at my side draw long and heavy breaths, the usual preliminaries to the bursting out of grief. This feeling, however, was but momentary; for Mary immediately said, "Charles and Henry and

Susan, you may now all come to me together ":
at the same time her hand was put into her
work-bag. We were at her side in an instant,
and in that time she held in her hand — what?
Not three little picture-books, but what was to
us a surprising novelty, viz., three little birds
wrought from sugar by the confectioner's art.
I had never seen or heard or dreamed of such a
thing. What a revulsion of delighted feeling
now swelled my little bosom! "If I should
give you books," said Mary, "you could not
read them at present; so I have got for you
what you will like better perhaps, and there
will be time enough for you to have books,
when you shall be able to read them. So, take
these little birds, and see how long you can
keep them." We were perfectly satisfied, and
even felt ourselves distinguished above the rest.
My bird was more to me than all the songsters
in the air, although it could not fly, or sing, or
open its mouth. I kept it for years, until by
accident it was crushed to pieces, and was no
longer a bird.

But Susan Clark — I was provoked at her.
Her bird was nothing to her but a piece of pep-
perminted sugar, and not a keepsake from Mary
Smith. She had not left the school-house
before she had nibbled off its bill.

The next summer, my present was the
" Death and Burial of Cock Robin." I could
then do something more than look at the
pictures. I could read the tragic history
which was told in verse below the pictured
representations of the mournful drama. How
I used to gaze and wonder at what I saw in
that little book! Could it be that all this really
took place; that the sparrow really did do the
murderous deed with his bow and his arrow?
I never knew before that birds had such things.
Then there was the fish with his dish, the rook
with his book, the owl with his shovel, &c. Yet,
if it were not all true, why should it be so pictured and related in the book? I had the impression that everything that was printed in a book
was surely true; and as no one thought to
explain to me the nature of a fable, I went on
puzzled and wondering, till progressive reason
at length divined its meaning. But Cock
Robin, with its red cover and gilded edges —
I have it now. It is the first little book I
ever received, and it was from Mary Smith;
and, as it is the only tangible memento of her
goodness that I possess, I shall keep it as long
as I can.

I had a similar present each successive
season, so long as I regularly attended the

summer school. What marvels did they con-
tain! How curiosity and wonder feasted on
their contents! They were mostly about giants,
fairies, witches, and ghosts. By this kind of
reading, superstition was trained up to a monstrous growth; and, as courage could not thrive
in its cold and gloomy shadow, it was a sickly
shoot for years. Giants, fairies, witches, and
ghosts were ready to pounce upon me from
every dark corner in the daytime, and from all
around in the night, if I happened to be alone.
I trembled to go to bed alone for years; and I
was often almost paralyzed with horror when
I chanced to wake in the stillness of midnight,
and my ever-busy fancy presented the grim and
grinning images with which I supposed darkness
to be peopled.

I wish I had all those little books now. I
would bequeath them to a national Lyceum, as
a specimen, or a mark to show what improvement has been made. Indeed, if improvement
has been made in anything, it has been in respect to children's books. When I compare
the world of fact in which the " Little Philoso-
phers " of the present day live, observe, and
enjoy, with the visionary regions where I
wandered, wondered, believed, and trembled,
I almost wish to be a child again, to know the

pleasure of having earliest curiosity fed with
fact, instead of fiction and folly, and to know
so much about the great world, with so young
a mind.

D

Chapter VIII

Grammar — Young Lady's Accidence
Murray — Parsing — Pope's Essay

ON my fifth summer, at the age of seven
and a half, I commenced the study of
grammar. The book generally used in our
school by beginners, was called the Young
Lady's Accidence. I had the honor of a new
one. The Young Lady's Accidence! How
often have I gazed on that last word, and
wondered what it meant! Even now, I cannot define it, though, of course, I have a guess
at its meaning. Let me turn this very minute
to that oracle of definitions, the venerable Webster: "A small book containing the rudiments
of grammar." That is it, then. But what an
intelligible and appropriate term for a little
child's book! The mysterious title, however,
was most appropriate to the contents of the
volume; for they were all mysterious, and that
for years, to my poor understanding.

Well, my first lesson was to get the Parts
of Speech, as they are called. What a grand

achievement to engrave on my memory these ten separate and strange words! With what ardor I took my lesson from the mistress, and trudged to my seat! It was a new study, and it was the first day of the school, moreover, before the bashfulness occasioned by a strange teacher had subsided, and before the spirit of play had been excited. So there was nothing at the moment to divert me from the lofty enterprise.

Reader, let your mind's eye peep into that old school-house. See that little boy in the second high seat from the front, in home-made and home-dyed pea-green cotton jacket and trowsers, with a clean Monday morning collar turned out from his neck. His new book is before him on the bench, kept open by his left hand. His right supports his head on its palm, with the corresponding elbow pressed on the bench. His lips move, but at first very slowly. He goes over the whole lesson in a low whisper. He now looks off his book, and pronounces two or three of the first, — article, noun, pronoun; then just glances at the page, and goes on with two or three more. He at length repeats several words without looking. Finally, he goes through the long catalogue, with his eye fastened on vacancy. At length, how his lips flutter, and you hear the parts of speech whizzing from his tongue like feathered arrows!

There, the rigmarole is accomplished. He starts up, and is at the mistress's side in a moment. "Will you hear my lesson, ma'am?" As she takes the book, he looks directly in her face, and repeats the aforementioned words loudly and distinctly, as if there were no fear of failure. He has got as far as the adverb; but now he hesitates, his eye drops, his lips are open ready for utterance, but the word does not come. He shuts them, he presses them hard together, he puts his finger to them, and there is a painful hiatus in his recitation, a disconnection, an *anti* to the very word he is after. "Conjunction," says the mistress. The little hand leaves the lips, at the same time that an involuntary "Oh!" bursts out from them. He lifts his head and his eye, and repeats with spirit the delinquent word, and goes on without hesitation to the end of the lesson. "Very well," says the teacher, or the hearer of the school; for she rather listened to than instructed her pupils. "Get so far for the next lesson." The child bows, whirls on his heel, and trips to his seat, mightily satisfied excepting with that one failure of memory, when that thundering word, *conjunction*, refused to come at his will.

But that word he never forgot again. The failure fastened it in his memory forever. This pea-green boy was myself, the present historian of the scene.

My next lesson lagged a little; my third seemed quite dull; my fourth I was two days in getting. At the end of the week, I thought that I could get along through the world very well without grammar, as my grandfather had done before me. But my mistress did not agree with me, and I was forced to go on. I contrived, however, to make easy work of the study. I got frequent, but very short lessons, only a single sentence at a time. This was easily committed to memory, and would stay on till I could run up and toss it off in recitation, after which it did not trouble me more. The recollection of it puts me in mind of a little boy lugging in wood, a stick at a time. My teacher was so ignorant of the philosophy of mind, that she did not know that this was not as good a way as any; and indeed, she praised me for my smartness. The consequence was, that, after I had been through the book, I could scarcely have repeated ten lines of it, excepting the very first and the very last lessons. Had it been ideas instead of words that had thus escaped from my mind, the case would have been different. As it was, the only matter of regret was, that I had been forming a bad habit, and had imbibed an erroneous notion, to wit, that lessons were to be learned simply to be recited.

The next winter this Accidence was committed, not to memory, but to oblivion; for, on presenting it to the master the first day of the school, he told me it was old-fashioned and out of date, and I must have Murray's Abridgment. So Murray was purchased, and I commenced the study of grammar again, excited by the novelty of a new and clean and larger book. But this soon became even more dull and dry than its predecessor; for it was more than twice the size, and the end of it was at the most discouraging distance of months, if not of years. I got only half way through the verb this winter. The next summer I began the book again, and arrived at the end of the account of the parts of speech. The winter after, I went over the same ground again, and got through the rules of syntax, and felt that I had accomplished a great work. The next summer I reviewed the whole grammar; for the mistress thought it necessary to have " its most practical and important parts firmly fixed in the memory, before attempting the higher exercises of the study." On the third winter, I began to apply my supposed knowledge in the process of *passing*, as it was termed by the master. The very pronunciation of this word shows how little the teacher exercised the power of independent thought. He had been accustomed to hear parse called *pass*; and, though the least reflection would have told him it was not correct, that reflection came not, and for years the grammarians of our district school *passed*. However, it was rightly so called. It *was* passing, as said exercise was performed; passing over, by, around, away, from the science of grammar, without coming near it, or at least without entering into it with much understanding of its nature. Mode, tense, case, government, and agreement were ever flying from our tongues, to be sure; but their meaning was as much a mystery as the hocus pocus of a juggler.

At first we parsed in simple prose, but soon entered on poetry. Poetry — a thing which to our apprehension differed from prose in this only, that each line began with a capital letter, and ended usually with a word sounding like another word at the end of the adjoining line. But, unskilled as we all generally were in the art of parsing, some of us came to think ourselves wonderfully acute and dexterous nevertheless. When we perceived the master himself to be in doubt and perplexity, then we felt ourselves on a level with him, and ventured to oppose our *guess* to his. And if he appeared a dunce extraordinary, as was sometimes the case, we used to put ourselves into the *potential* mood pretty often, as we knew that our teacher could never assume the *imperative* on this subject.

The fact is, neither we nor the teacher entered into the writer's meaning. The general plan of the work was not surveyed, nor the particular sense of separate passages examined. We could not do it, perhaps from the want of maturity of mind; the teacher did not, because he had never been accustomed to anything of the kind in his own education; and it never occurred to him that he could deviate from the track, or improve upon the methods of those who taught him. Pope's Essay on Man was the parsing manual used by the most advanced. No wonder, then, that pupil and pedagogue so often got bewildered and lost in a world of thought like this; for, however well ordered a creation it might be, it was scarcely better than a chaos to them.

In closing, I ought to remark, that all our teachers were not thus ignorant of grammar, although they did not perhaps take the best way to teach it. In speaking thus of this department of study, and also of others, I have reference to the more general character of schoolmasters and schools.

Chapter IX

The Particular Master—Various Methods of Punishment

I HAVE given some account of my first winter at school. Of my second, third, and fourth, I have nothing of importance to say. The routine was the same in each. The teachers were remarkable for nothing in particular: if they were, I have too indistinct a remembrance of their characters to portray them now ; so I will pass them by, and describe the teacher of my fifth.

He was called the *particular* master. The scholars in speaking of him, would say, " He is so particular." The first morning of the school, he read us a long list of regulations to be observed in school, and out. " There are more rules than you could shake a stick at before your arm would ache," said some one. " And if the master should shake a stick at every one who should disobey them, he would not find time to do much else," said another. Indeed, it proved to be so. Half the time was spent in calling up scholars for little misdemeanors, trying to make them confess their faults, and promise stricter obedience, or in devising punishments and inflicting them. Almost every method was tried that was ever suggested to the brain of pedagogue. Some were feruled on the hand; some were whipped with a rod on the back; some were compelled to hold out, at arm's length, the largest book which could be found, or a great leaden inkstand, till muscle and nerve, bone and marrow, were tortured with the continued exertion. If the arm bent or inclined from the horizontal level, it was forced back again by a knock of the ruler on the elbow. I well recollect that one poor fellow forgot his suffering by fainting quite away. This lingering punishment was more befitting the vengeance of a savage, than the corrective efforts of a teacher of the young in civilized life.

He had recourse to another method, almost, perhaps quite, as barbarous. It was standing in a stooping posture, with the finger on the head of a nail in the floor. It was a position not particularly favorable to health of body or soundness of mind; the head being brought about as low as the knees, the blood rushing to it, and pressing unnaturally on the veins, often caused a dull pain, and a staggering dizziness. That man's judgment or mercy must have been topsy-turvy also, who first set the example of such an infliction on those whose progress in knowledge depended somewhat on their being kept right end upward.

The above punishments were sometimes rendered doubly painful by their taking place directly in front of the enormous fire, so that the pitiable culprit was roasted as well as racked. Another mode of punishment — an anti-whispering process — was setting the jaws at a painful distance apart, by inserting a chip perpendicularly between the teeth. Then we occasionally had our hair pulled, our noses tweaked, our ears pinched and boxed, or snapped, perhaps, with India-rubber; this last the perfection of eartingling operations. There were minor penalties, moreover, for minor faults. The uneasy urchins were clapped into the closet, thrust under the desk, or perched on its top. Boys were made to sit in the girls' seats, amusing the school with their grinning awkwardness; and girls were obliged to sit on the masculine side of the aisle, with crimsoned necks, and faces buried in their aprons.

But I have dwelt long enough on the various penalties of the numerous violations of Master

Particular's many orders.   After all, he did not
keep an orderly school.   The cause of the mischief was, he was variable.   He wanted that
persevering firmness and uniformity which alone
can insure success.   He had so many regulations, that he could not stop at all times to
notice the transgressions of them.   The scholars, not knowing with certainty what to expect,
dared to run the risk of disobedience.   The
consequence of this procedure on the part of
the ruler and the ruled was, that the school
became uncommonly riotous before the close
of the season.   The larger scholars soon broke
over all restraint; but the little ones were nar-
rowly watched and restricted somewhat longer.
But these gradually grew unmindful of the un-
stable authority, and finally contemned it with
almost insolent effrontery, unless the master's
temper-kindled eye was fixed directly and men-
acingly upon them.   Thus the many regulations were like so many cobwebs, through which
the great flies would break at once, and so tear
and disorder the net that it would not hold even
the little ones, or at all answer the purpose for
which it was spun.

I would not have it understood that this
master was singular in his punishments; for
such methods of correcting offenders have been

in use time out of mind.   He was distinguished
only for resorting to them more frequently
than any other instructor within my own observation.   The truth is, that it seemed to be the
prevailing opinion both among teachers and
parents, that boys and girls *would* play and be
mischievous at any rate, and that consequently
masters *must* punish in some way or other.
It was a matter of course; nothing better
was expected.

Chapter X

How they used to read in the Old School-house in District No. V

IN this description of the District School, as it *was*, that frequent and important exercise, Reading, must not be omitted, — Reading as it *was*. Advance, then, ye readers of the Old School-house, and let us witness your performances.

We will suppose it is the first day of the school. "Come and read," says the mistress to a little flaxen-headed creature of doubtful gender; for the child is in petticoats, and sits on the female side, as close as possible to a guardian sister. But then those coarser features, tanned complexion, and close-clipped hair, with other minutiæ of aspect, are somewhat contradictory to the feminine dress. "Come and read." It is the first time that this he or she was ever inside of a school-house, and in the presence of a school-ma'am, according to recollection, and the order is heard with shrinking timidity. But the sister whispers an encouraging word, and helps "tot" down from the seat, who creeps out into the aisle, and hesitates along down to the teacher, biting his fingers, or scratching his head, perhaps both, to relieve the embarrassment of the novel situation. "What is your name, dear?" "*Tholomon Icherthon*," lisps the now-discovered he, in a phlegm-choked voice, scarce above a whisper. "Put your hands down by your side, Solomon, and make a bow." He obeys, if a short and hasty jerk of the head is a bow. The alphabetical page of the spelling-book is presented, and he is asked, "What's that?" But he cannot tell. He is but two years and a half old, and has been sent to school to relieve his mother from trouble, rather than to learn. No one at home has yet shown or named a letter to him. He has never had even that celebrated character, round O, pointed out to his notice. It was an older beginner, most probably, who, being asked a similar question about the first letter of the alphabet, replied, "I know him by sight, but can't tell him by name." But our namesake of the wise man does not know the gentleman even by sight, nor any of his twenty-five companions.

Solomon Richardson has at length said A, B, C, for the first time in his life. He has *read*.

" That's a nice boy; make another bow, and go to your seat." He gives another jerk of the head, and whirls on his heel, and trots back to his seat, meeting the congratulatory smile of his sister with a satisfied grin, which, put into language, would be, " There, I've read, ha'nt I ? "

The little chit, at first so timid, and almost inaudible in enunciation, in a few days becomes accustomed to the place and the exercise; and, in obedience to the " Speak up loud, that's a good boy," he soon pipes off *A-er*, *B-er*, *C-er*, &c., with a far-ringing shrillness, that vies even with chanticleer himself. Solomon went all the pleasant days of the first summer, and nearly every day of the next, before he knew all the letters by sight, or could call them by name. Strange that it should take so long to become acquainted with these twenty-six characters, when, in a month's time, the same child becomes familiar with the forms and the names of hundreds of objects in nature around, or in use about his father's house, shop, or farm! Not so very strange either, if we only reflect a moment. Take a child into a party of twenty-six persons, all strangers, and lead him from one to the other as fast as his little feet can patter, telling him their respective names, all

E

in less than ten minutes; do this four times a day even, and you would not be surprised if he should be weeks at least, if not months, in learning to designate them all by their names. Is it any matter of surprise, then, that the child should be so long in becoming acquainted with the alphabetical party, when he is introduced to them precisely in the manner above described? Then, these are not of different heights, complexions, dresses,· motions, and tones of voice, as a living company have. But there they stand in an unalterable line, all in the same complexions and dress; all just so tall, just so motionless and mute and uninteresting, and, of course, the most unrememberable figures in the world. No wonder that some should go to school, and "sit on a bench, and say A B C," as a little girl said, for a whole year, and still find themselves strangers to some of the sable company, even then. Our little reader is permitted at length to turn a leaf, and he finds himself in the region of the Abs, — an expanse of little syllables, making me, who am given to comparisons, think of an extensive plain whereon there is no tree or shrub or plant, or anything else inviting to the eye, and nothing but little stones, stones, stones, all about the same size. And what must the poor

little learner do here? Why, he must hop from
cobble to cobble, if I may so call *ab*, *eb*, *ib*, as
fast as he possibly can, naming each one, after
the voice of the teacher, as he hurries along.
And this must be kept up until he can denomi-
nate each lifeless and uninteresting object on
the face of the desert.

After more or less months, the weary novice
ceases to be an Ab-ite. He is next put into
whole words of one syllable, arranged in columns. The first word we read in Perry that
conveyed anything like an idea, was the first
one in the first column, — the word *ache :* ay,
we did not easily forget what this meant, when
once informed; the corresponding idea, or rather
feeling, was so often in our consciousness. *Ache*,
— a very appropriate term with which to begin
a course of education so abounding in pains of
body and of mind.

After five pages of this perpendicular reading,
if I may so call it, we entered on the horizontal, that is, on words arranged in sentences and
paragraphs. This was reading in good earnest,
as grown-up folks did, and something with
which tiny childhood would be very naturally
puffed up. "Easy Lessons" was the title of
about a dozen separate chapters, scattered at
intervals among the numerous spelling columns,

like brambly openings here and there amid the tall forest. Easy lessons, because they consisted mostly of little monosyllabic words, easy to be pronounced. But they were not easy as it regards being understood. They were made up of abstract moral sentences, presenting but a very faint meaning to the child, if any at all. Their particular application to his own conduct he would not perceive, of course, without help; and this it scarcely ever entered the head or the heart of the teacher to afford.

In the course of summers, how many I forget, we arrived at the most manly and dignified reading the illustrious Perry had prepared for us. It was entitled "Moral Tales and Fables." In these latter, beasts and birds talked like men; and strange sorts of folks, called Jupiter, Mercury, and Juno, were pictured as sitting up in the clouds, and talking with men and animals on earth, or as down among them doing very unearthly things. To quote language in common use, we *kind o' believed it all to be true, and yet we kind o' didn't.* As for the "moral" at the end, teachers never dreamed of attracting our attention to it. Indeed, we had no other idea of all these Easy Lessons, Tales, and Fables, than that they were to be syllabled from the tongue in the task of reading. That they were to sink into the heart, and make us better in life, never occurred to our simple understandings.

Among all the rest were five pieces of poetry, — charming stuff to read ; the words would come along one after another so easily, and the lines would jingle so pleasantly together at the end, tickling the ear like two beads in a rattle. " Oh ! give us poetry to read, of all things," we thought.

We generally passed directly from the spelling-book to the reading-book of the first class, although we were ranked the second class still. Or perhaps we took a book which had been formerly used by the first class ; for a new reading-book was generally introduced once in a few years in compliance with the earnest recommendation of the temporary teacher. While the first class were in Scott's Lessons, we of the second were pursuing their tracks, not altogether understandingly, through Adams' Understanding Reader. When a new master persuaded them into Murray, then we were admitted into Scott.

The principal requisites in reading, in these days, were to read fast, mind the " stops and marks," and speak up loud. As for suiting the tone to the meaning, no such thing was dreamed of, in our school at least. As much emphasis was laid on an insignificant *of* or *and* as on the most important word in the piece. But no wonder we did not know how to vary our tones, for we did not always know the meaning of the words, or enter into the general spirit of the composition. This was very frequently, indeed almost always, the case with the majority even of the first class. Parliamentary prose and Miltonic verse were just about as good as Greek for the purpose of modulating the voice according to meaning. It scarcely ever entered the heads of our teachers to question us about the ideas hidden in the great, long words and spacious sentences. It is possible that they did not always discover it themselves. " Speak up there, and not read like a mouse in a cheese ; and mind your stops," — such were the principal directions respecting the important art of elocution. Important it was most certainly considered ; for each class must read twice in the forenoon, and the same in the afternoon, from a quarter to half an hour each time, according to the size of the class. Had they read but once or twice, and but little at a time, and this with nice and very profitable attention to tone and sense, parents would have thought the master most miserably deficient in duty, and their children cheated out of their rights, notwithstanding

the time thus saved should be most assiduously
devoted to other all-important branches of education.

It ought not to be omitted, that the Bible,
particularly the New Testament, was the reading twice a day, generally, for all the classes
adequate to words of more than one syllable.
It was the only reading of several of the younger
classes under some teachers. On this practice
I shall make but a single remark. As far as
my own experience and observation extended,
reverence for the sacred volume was not deep-
ened by this constant but exceedingly careless
use.

Chapter XI

How they used to spell

THERE, the class have read; but they have
something else to do before they take
their seats. "Shut your books," says he who
has been hearing them read. What makes this
row of little countenances brighten up so suddenly, especially the upper end of it? What
wooden faces and leaden eyes, two minutes
ago! The reading was nothing to them, —
those select sentences and maxims in Perry's
spelling-book which are tucked in between the
fables. It is all as dull as a dirge to those life-
loving boys and girls. They almost drowsed
while they stood up in their places. But they
are fully awake now. They are going to spell.
But this in itself is the driest exercise to pre-
pare for, and the driest to perform, of the
whole round. The child cares no more in his
heart about the arrangement of vowels and
consonants in the orthography of words, than
he does how many chips lie one above another
at the school-house wood-pile. But he does

care whether he is at the head or foot of his
class; whether the money dangles from his own
neck or another's. This is the secret of the
interest in spelling. Emulation is awakened,
ambition roused. There is something like the
tug of strength in the wrestle, something of
the alternation of hope and fear in a game of
chance. There has been a special preparation
for the trial. Observe this class any day, half
an hour before they are called up to read. What
a flitting from top to bottom of the spelling
column, and what a flutter of lips and hissing
of utterance! Now the eye twinkles on the
page to catch a word, and now it is fixed on
the empty air, while the orthography is syllabled over and over again in mind, until at
length it is syllabled on the memory. But the
time of trial has come; they have only to read
first. "The third class may come and read."
"O dear, I haven't got my spelling lesson,"
mutters Charlotte to herself. She has just
begun the art of writing this winter, and she
lingered a little too long at her hooks and trammels. The lesson seems to her to have as
many again hard words in it as common.
What a flutter she is in! She got up above
George in the forenoon, and she would not get
down again for anything. She is as slow in

coming from her seat as she possibly can be
and keep moving. She makes a chink in her
book with her finger, and every now and then,
during the reading exercise, steals a glance at a
difficult word.

But the reading is over, and what a brighten-
ing up, as was said before, with the exception,
perhaps, of two or three idle or stupid boys at
that less honorable extremity of the class called
the foot! That boy at the head — no, it *was*
a boy; but Harriet has at length got above
him; and, when girls once get to the head, get
them away from it if you can. Once put the
"pride of place" into their hearts, and how
they will queen it! Then they are more sensitive regarding anything that might lower
them in the eyes of others, and seem the least
like disgrace. I have known a little girl to cry
the half of one day, and look melancholy the
whole of the next, on losing her place at the
head. Girls are more likely to arrive at and
keep the first place in the class, in consequence
of a little more help from mother nature than
boys get. I believe that they generally have a
memory more fitted for catching and holding
words and other signs addressed to the eye,
than the other sex. That girl at the head has
studied her spelling lesson, until she is as con-

fident of every word as the unerring Perry himself. She can spell every word in the column,
in the order it stands, without the master's
" putting it out," she has been over it so many
times. " Now, Mr. James, get up again if you
can," thinks Harriet. I pity you, poor girl;
for James has an ally that will blow over your
proud castle in the air. Old Boreas, the king
of the winds, will order out a snow-storm by
and by, to block up the roads, so that none
but booted and weather-proof males can get to
school; and you, Miss, must lose a day or two,
and then find yourself at the foot with those
blockhead boys who always abide there. But
let it not be thought that all those foot lads are
deficient in intellect. Look at them when the
master's back is turned, and you will see mischievous ingenuity enough to convince you that
they might surpass even James and Harriet, had
some other faculties been called into exercise
besides the mere memory of verbalities.

The most extraordinary spelling, and indeed
reading machine, in our school, was a boy whom
I shall call Memorus Wordwell. He was
mighty and wonderful in the acquisition and
remembrance of words, — of signs without the
ideas signified. The alphabet he acquired at
home before he was two years old. What exul-

tation of parents, what exclamation from admiring visitors! "There was never anything like it." He had almost accomplished his Abs before he was thought old enough for school. At an earlier age than usual, however, he was sent; and then he went from *Ache* to *Abomination* in half the summers and winters it took the rest of us to go over the same space. Astonishing how quickly he mastered column after column, section after section, of obstinate orthographies. Those martial terms I have just used, together with our hero's celerity, put me in mind of Cæsar. So I will quote him. Memorus might have said in respect to the host of the spelling-book, "I came, I saw, I conquered." He generally stood at the head of a class, each one of whom was two years his elder. Poor creatures! they studied hard, some of them, but it did no good: Memorus Wordwell was born to be above them, as some men are said to have been "born to command." At the public examination of his first winter, the people of the district, and even the minister, thought it marvelous that such monstrous great words should be mastered by "such a leetle mite of a boy!" Memorus was mighty also in saying those after spelling matters — the Key, the Abbreviations, the Punctuation, &c. These things were deemed of

great account to be laid up in remembrance,
although they were all very imperfectly understood, and some of them not understood at all.

Punctuation — how many hours, days, and
even weeks, have I tugged away to lift, as it
were, to roll up into the store-house of my
memory, the many long, heavy sentences com-
prehended under this title ! Only survey (we
use this word when speaking of considerable
space and bulk) — only survey the first sentence,
a transcript of which I will endeavor to locate
in these narrow bounds. I would have my
readers of the rising generation know what
mighty labors we little creatures of five, six, and
seven years old were set to perform : —

" Punctuation is the art of pointing, or of
dividing a discourse into periods by points, expressing the pauses to be made in the reading
thereof, and regulating the cadence or elevation
of the voice."

There, I have labored weeks on that; for I
always had the lamentable defect of mind not
to be able to commit to memory what I did not
understand. My teachers never aided me with
the least explanation of the above-copied sentence, nor of other reading of a similar character,
which was likewise to be committed to memory.
But this and all was nothing, as it were, to

Memorus Wordwell.   He was a very Hercules
in this wilderness of words.

Master Wordwell was a remarkable reader
too.   He could rattle off a word as extensive as
the name of a Russian noble, when he was but
five years old, as easily as the schoolmaster himself.   " He can read in the hardest chapters of
the Testament as fast agin as I can," said his
mother.   " I never did see nothin beat it," exclaimed his father; " he speaks up as loud as a
minister."   But I have said enough about this
prodigy.   I have said thus much, because, although he was thought so surpassingly bright, he
was the most decided ninny in the school.   The
fact is, he did not know what the sounds he
uttered meant.   It never entered his head, nor
the heads of his parents and most of his teachers,
that words and sentences were written, and
should be read, only to be understood.   He lost
some of his reputation, however, when he grew
up towards twenty-one, and it was found that
numbers, in more senses than one, were far above
him in arithmetic.

One little anecdote about Memorus Wordwell before we let him go, and this long chapter
shall be no longer.

It happened one day that the " cut and split "
for the fire fell short, and Jonas Patch was out

wielding the ax in school time. He had been at work about half an hour, when Memorus, who was perceived to have less to do than the rest, was sent out to take his place. He was about ten years old, and four years younger than Jonas. "Memorus, you may go out and spell Jonas." Our hero did not think of the Yankee sense in which the master used the word *spell*: indeed he had never attached but one meaning to it, whenever it was used with reference to himself. He supposed the master was granting him a ride extraordinary on his favorite hobby. So he put his spelling-book under his arm, and was out at the wood-pile with the speed of a boy rushing to play.

"Ye got yer spellin lesson, Jonas?" was his first salutation. "Haven't looked at it yit," was the reply. "I mean to cut up this plaguy great log, spellin or no spellin, before I go in. I had as lieve keep warm here choppin wood, as freeze up there in that tarnal cold back seat." "Well, the master sent me out to hear you spell." "Did he? well, put out the words, and I'll spell." Memorus being so distinguished a speller, Jonas did not doubt but that he was really sent out on this errand. So our deputy spelling-master mounted the top of the wood-pile, just in front of Jonas, to put out words to his temporary pupil, who still kept on putting out chips.

"Do you know where the lesson begins, Jonas?" "No, I don't; but I 'spose I shall find out now." "Well, here 'tis." (They both belonged to the same class.) "Spell A-bom-i-na-tion." Jonas spells. A-b-o-m bom a-bom (in the mean time up goes the ax high in air), i a-bom-i (down it goes again chuck into the wood) n-a na a-bom-i-na (up it goes again) t-i-o-n tion, a-bom-i-na-tion; chuck the ax goes again, and at the same time out flies a furious chip, and hits Memorus on the nose. At this moment the master appeared just at the corner of the school-house, with one foot still on the threshold. "Jonas, why don't you come in? didn't I send Memorus out to spell you?" "Yes, sir, and he has been spelling me; how could I come in if he spelt me here?" At this the master's eye caught Memorus perched up on the top-stick, with his book open upon his lap, rubbing his nose, and just in the act of putting out the next word of the column. Ac-com-mo-da-tion, pronounced Memorus in a broken but louder voice than before; for he had caught a glimpse of the master, and he wished to let him know that he was doing his duty. This was too much for the master's gravity.

He perceived the mistake, and, without saying
more, wheeled back into the school-room, almost
bursting with the most tumultuous laughter he
ever tried to suppress.   The scholars wondered
at his looks, and grinned in sympathy.   But in
a few minutes Jonas came in, followed by
Memorus with his spelling-book, who exclaimed,
" I have heard him spell clean through the
whole lesson, and he didn't spell hardly none of
'em right."   The master could hold in no
longer, and the scholars perceived the blunder,
and there was one simultaneous roar from pedagogue and pupils; the scholars laughing twice
as loud and uproariously in consequence of being
permitted to laugh in school time, and to do it
with the accompaniment of the master.

F

Chapter XII

Mr. Spoutsound, the Speaking Master — the Exhibition

NOW comes winter the sixth, of my district education. Our master was as insignificant a personage as is often met with beyond the age of twenty-one. He ought to have been pedagogue in that land of littleness, Lilliput. Our great fellows of the back seat might have tossed him out of the window from the palm of the hand. But he possessed certain qualifications, and pursued such a course that he was permitted to retain the magisterial seat through his term, and indeed was quite popular on the whole.

He was as remarkable for the loudness and compass of his voice, as for the diminutiveness of his material dimensions. How such a body of sound could proceed from so bodiless an existence, was a marvel. It seemed as unnatural as that a tremendous thunder-clap should burst from a speck of cloud in the sky. He gener-

ally sat with the singers on the Sabbath, and
drowned the feebler voices with the inundation
of his bass.

But it was not with his tuneful powers alone,
that he "astonished the natives." He was
imagined to possess great gifts of oratory likewise. " What a pity it is that he had not been
a minister ! " was said. It was by his endow-
ments and taste in this respect that he made
himself particularly memorable in our school.
Mr. Spoutsound had been one quarter, to an
academy where declamation was a weekly exercise. Finding in this, ample scope for his vocal
extraordinariness (a long-winded word, to be
sure, but so appropriate), he became an enthusi-
astic votary to the Ciceronian art. The principal qualification of an orator in his view, was
height, depth, and breadth of utterance, — quan-
tity of sound. Of course, he fancied himself a
very lion in oratory. Indeed, as far as roaring
would go, he was a lion. This gentleman introduced declamation, or the speaking of pieces,
as it was called, into our school. He considered
" speaking of the utmost consequence in this
country, as any boy might be called to a seat
in the legislature, perhaps, in the course of
things." It was a novelty to the scholars, and
they entered with their whole souls into the

matter. It was a pleasant relief to the dullness
of the old-fashioned routine.

What a rummaging of books, pamphlets, and
newspapers now took place, to find pieces to
speak! The American Preceptor, the Colum-
bian Orator, the Art of Reading, Scott's Elocution, Webster's Third Part, and I know not
how many other ancients, were taken down
from their dusty retirement at home, for the sake
of the specimens of eloquence they afforded.
Those pieces were deemed best by us grandsons
of the Revolutionists, which most abounded in
those glorious words, Freedom, Liberty, Inde-
pendence, and other spirit-kindling names and
phrases, that might be mentioned. Another
recommendation was high-flown language, and
especially words that were long and sonorous,
such as would roll thunderingly from the tongue.
For, like our district professor, we had the impression that noise was the most important
quality in eloquence. The first, the second,
and the third requisite was the same; it was
noise, noise, noise. Action, however, or gesticulation, was not omitted. This was considered
the next qualification of a good orator. So
there was the most vehement swinging of arms,
shaking of fists, and waving of palms. That
occasional motion of the limb and force of

voice, called emphasis, was not a characteristic
of our eloquence, or rather it was all emphasis.
Our utterance was something like the continuous roar of a swollen brook over a mill-dam,
and our action like the unintermitted whirling
and clapping of adjacent machinery.

We tried our talent in the dramatic way likewise. There were numerous extracts from
dramatic compositions scattered through the
various reading-books we had mustered. These
dialogistic performances were even more interesting than our speechifying in the semblance
of lawyers and legislators. We more easily
acquired an aptitude for this exercise, as it was
somewhat like that every-day affair, conversation. In this we were brought face to face,
voice to voice, with each other, and our social
sympathies were kindled into glow. We talked
with, as well as at, folks. Then the female
portion of the school could take a part in the
performance; and who does not know that dialoguing, as well as dancing, has twice the zest
with a female partner? The whole school, with
the exception of the very least perhaps, were
engaged, indeed absorbed, in this novel branch
of education introduced by Mr. Spoutsound.
Some, who had not got out of their Abs, were
taught, by admiring fathers and mothers at

home, little pieces by rote, and made to screech
them out with most ear-splitting execution.
One lad in this way committed to memory that
famous piece of self-puffery beginning with the
lines, —

> " You'd scarce expect one of my age
> To speak in public on the stage."

Memorus Wordwell committed to memory
and parroted forth that famous speech of Pitt,
in which he so eloquently replies to the charge
of being a young man.

Cicero at Athens was not more assiduous in
seeking the "immense and the infinite " in eloquence, than we were in seeking the great in
speaking.   Besides half an hour of daily school
time set apart for the exercise, under the immediate direction and exemplification of the master,
our noonings were devoted to the same, as far
as the young's ruling passion, the love of play,
would permit.   And on the way to and from
school, the pleasure of dialogue would compete
with that of dousing each other into the snow.
We even " spoke " while doing our night and
morning work at home.   A boy might be seen
at the wood-pile hacking at a log and a dialogue
by turns.   Or perhaps, after dispensing the
fodder to the tenants of the barn, he would

mount a half-cleared scaffold, and out-bellow the wondering beeves below.

As the school drew towards a close, Mr. Spoutsound proposed to have an exhibition in addition to the usual examination, on the last day, or rather the evening of it. Our oratorical gifts and accomplishments must be publicly displayed; which is next to publicly using them in the important affairs of the town, the State, or the country.

"An exhibition!—I want to know! can it be?" There had never been anything like it in the district before, nor indeed in the town. Such a thing had scarcely been heard of, except by some one whose uncle or cousin had been to the academy or to college. The people of the district were wide awake. The younger portion of them could hardly sleep nights.

The scholars are requested to select the pieces they would prefer to speak, whether speeches or dialogues; and to arrange among themselves who should be fellow-partners in the dramatical performances. The master, however, retained the right of veto on their choice. Now, what a rustle of leaves and flutter of lips in school-hours, and noisier flapping of books and clatter of tongues at noon, in settling who shall have which, and who speak with whom. At length all is arranged, and mostly to the minds of all. Then, for a week or two before the final consummation of things eloquent, it was nothing but rehearsal. No pains were spared by any one that he might be perfect in the recollection and flourishing-off of his part. Dialoguists were grouped together in every corner. There was a buzz in the back seat, a hum in the closet, a screech in the entry, and the very climax of vociferation in the spelling-floor. Here the solos (if I may borrow a term from music) were rehearsed under the immediate criticism of Mr. Spoutsound, whose chief delight was in forensic and parliamentary eloquence. The old schoolhouse was a little Babel in the confusion of tongues.

The expected day at length arrives. There must be, of course, the usual examination in the afternoon. But nobody attended this but the minister, and the committee who engaged the master. The people of the district all intended to be at the exhibition in the evening, and examination was " just nothing at all " with that in prospect. And, in fact, it *was* just nothing at all; for the " ruling passion " had swallowed up very much of the time that should have been devoted to the really important branches of education.

After the finishing of the school, a stage was erected at the end of the spelling-floor, next to the desk and the closet. It was hung round with checked bed-blankets, in the semblance of theatrical curtains, to conceal any preparations that might be necessary between the pieces.

The exhibition was to commence at half past six. Before that time, the old school-house was crowded to the utmost of its capacity for containing, by the people not only of our district, but of other parts of the town. The children were wedged into chinks too narrow for the admission of the grown-up. Never were a multitude of living bodies more completely compressed and amalgamated into one continuous mass.

On the front writing-bench, just before the stage, and facing the audience, sat the four first, and some of the most interesting performers on the occasion, viz., players on the clarionet, violin, bass-viol, and bassoon. But they of the bow were sorely troubled at first. Time and space go together with them, you know. They cannot keep the first without possessing the latter. As they sat, their semibreves were all shortened into minims, indeed into crotchets, for lack of elbow-room. At length the violinist stood up straight on the writing-bench,

so as to have an unimpeded stretch in the
empty air, above the thicket of heads. His
fellow-sufferer then contrived to stand so that
his long bow could sweep freely between the
steady heads of two broad-shouldered men, out
of danger from joggling boys. This band dis-
coursed what was to our ears most eloquent
music, as a prelude to the musical eloquence
which was to be the chief entertainment of the
occasion. They played intermediately also, and
gave the winding-off flourish of sound.

At forty minutes past six, the curtain rose;
that is, the bed-blankets were pulled aside.
There stood Mr. Spoutsound on the stage, in
all the pomp possible to diminutiveness. He
advanced two steps, and bowed as profoundly
from height to depth as his brevity of stature
would admit. He then opened the exhibition
by speaking a poetical piece called a Prologue,
which he found in one of the old reading-books.
As this was originally composed as an introduction to a stage performance, it was thought
appropriate on this occasion. Mr. Spoutsound
now put forth in all the plenitude of his utterance. It seemed a vocal cataract, all torrent,
thunder, and froth. But it wanted room, — an
abyss to empty into; and all it had was the
remnant of space left in our little school-room.

A few of the audience were overwhelmed with the pour and rush and roar of the pent-up noise, and the rest with admiration, yea, astonishment, that the schoolmaster " *could speak so.*"

He ceased — it was all as still as if every other voice had died of envy. He bowed — there was then a general breathing, as if the vocals were just coming to life again. He sat down on a chair placed on the stage; then there was one general buzz, above which arose, here and there, a living and loud voice. Above this, soon arose the exaltation of the orator's favorite march; for he deemed it proper that his own performance should be separated from those of his pupils by some length and loftiness of music.

Now the exhibition commenced in good earnest. The dramatists dressed in costumes according to the character to be sustained, as far as all the old and odd dresses that could be mustered up would enable them to do so. The district, and indeed the town, had been ransacked for revolutionary coats and cocked-up hats and other grand-fatherly and grand-motherly attire.

The people present were quite as much amused with the spectacle as with the speaking. To see the old fashions on the young folks, and to see the young folks personating characters so entirely opposite to their own; for instance, the slim, pale-faced youth, by the aid of stuffing, looking, and acting the fat old wine-bibber; the blooming girl of seventeen, putting on the cap, the kerchief, and the character of seventy-five, &c., — all this was ludicrously strange. A very refined taste might have observed other things that were strangely ludicrous in the elocution and gesticulation of these disciples of Mr. Spout-sound; but most of the company present were so fortunate as to perceive no bad taste to mar their enjoyment.

The little boy of five spoke the little piece —

"You'd scarce expect one of my age," &c.

I recollect another line of the piece which has become singularly verified in the history of the lad. It is this —

"Tall oaks from little acorns grow."

Now, this acorn of eloquence, which sprouted forth so vigorously on this occasion, has at length grown into a mighty oak of oratory on his native hills. He has flourished in a Fourth of July oration before his fellow-townsmen.

Memorus Wordwell, who at this time was eleven years old, yelped forth the aforementioned speech of Pitt. In the part replying to the

taunt that the author of the speech was a young
man, Memorus " beat all." Next to the master himself, he excited the greatest admiration,
and particularly in his father and mother.

But this chapter must be ended, so we will
skip to the end of this famous exhibition. At
a quarter past ten, the curtain dropped for the
last time; that is, the bed-blankets were pulled
down and put into the sleighs of their owners,
to be carried home to be spread over the
dreamers of acts, instead of being hung before
the actors of dreams. The little boys and girls
did not get to bed till eleven o'clock that night,
nor all of them to sleep till twelve. They were
never more the pupils of Mr. Spoutsound. He
soon migrated to one of the States beyond the
Alleghany. There he studied law not more
than a year certainly, and was admitted to the
Bar. It is rumored that he soon *spoke* himself
into the legislature, and as soon spoke himself
out again. Whether he will speak himself into
Congress is a matter of exceeding doubt. I
have nothing more to add respecting the speaking master, or the speaking, excepting that one
shrewd old man was heard to say on leaving the
school-house, exhibition night, "A great *cry*, but
little wool."

Chapter XIII

Learning to write

THE winter I was nine years old, I made another advance toward the top of the ladder, in the circumstance of learning to write. I desired and pleaded to commence the chirographical art the summer, and indeed the winter before; for others of my own age were at it thus early. But my father said that my fingers were hardly stout enough to manage a quill from his geese; but that, if I would put up with the quill of a hen, I might try. This pithy satire put an end to my teasing.

Having previously had the promise of writing this winter, I had made all the necessary preparations, days before school was to begin. I had bought me a new birch ruler, and had given a third of my wealth, four cents, for it. To this I had appended, by a well-twisted flaxen string, a plummet of my own running, whittling, and scraping. I had hunted up an old pewter inkstand, which had come down from the ancestral eminence of my great grandfather, for aught I know; and it bore many marks of a speedier and less honorable descent, to wit, from table or desk to the floor. I had succeeded in becoming the owner of a penknife, not that it was likely to be applied to its appropriate use that winter at least; for such beginners generally used the instrument to mar that kind of pens they wrote in, rather than to make or mend those they wrote with. I had selected one of the fairest quills out of an enormous bunch. Half a quire of foolscap had been folded into the shape of a writing-book by the maternal hand, and covered with brown paper, nearly as thick as a sheepskin.

Behold me now, on the first Monday in December, starting for school, with my new and clean writing-book buttoned under my jacket, my inkstand in my pocket, a bundle of necessary books in one hand, and my ruler and swinging plummet in the other, which I flourished in the air and around my head, till the sharpened lead made its first mark on my own face. My long white-feathered goose-quill was twisted into my hat-band, like a plumy badge of the distinction to which I had arrived, and the important enterprise before me.

On arriving at the school-house, I took a seat higher up and more honorable than the

one I occupied the winter before. At the
proper time, my writing-book, which, with my
quill, I had handed to the master on entering,
was returned to me, with a copy set, and paper
ruled and pen made. My copy was a single
straight mark, at the first corner of my manuscript. "A straight mark! who could not
make so simple a thing as that?" thought I.
I waited, however, to see how the boy next to
me, a beginner also, should succeed, as he had
got ready a moment before me. Never shall
I forget the first chirographical exploit of this
youth. That inky image will never be eradi-
cated from my memory, so long as a single
trace of early experience is left on its tablet.
The fact is, it was an epoch in my life: something great was to be done, and my attention
was intensely awake to whatever had a bearing
on this new and important trial of my powers.
I looked to see a mark as straight as a ruler,
having its four corners as distinctly defined as
the angles of a parallelogram.

But, O me! what a spectacle! What a
shocking contrast to my anticipation! That
mark had as many crooks as a ribbon in the
wind, and nearer eight angles than four; and
its two sides were nearly as rough and as
notched as a fine handsaw; and, indeed, the

mark somewhat resembled it in width, for the
fellow had laid in a store of ink sufficient to
last the journey of the whole line. "Shame
on him!" said I, internally, "I can beat that,
I know." I began by setting my pen firmly
on the paper, and I brought a mark half way
down with rectilinear precision. But by this
time my head began to swim, and my hand
to tremble. I was as it were in vacancy, far
below the upper ruling, and as far above the
lower. My self-possession failed; my pen
diverged to the right, then to the left, crook-
ing all the remainder of its way, with as many
zig-zags as could well be in so short a distance.
Mine was as sad a failure as my neighbor's. I
covered it over with my fingers, and did not jog
him with a "see there," as I had vainly anticipated.

So much for painstaking, now for chance.
By good luck the next effort was quite success-
ful. I now dashed on, for better or worse, till
in one half-hour I had covered the whole page
with the standing, though seemingly falling,
monuments of the chirographical wisdom of
my teacher, and skill of myself. In the afternoon a similar copy was set, and I dashed on
again as if I had taken so much writing by the
job, and my only object was to save time. Now

G

and then there was quite a reputable mark; but alas — for him whose perception of the beautiful was particularly delicate, should he get a glimpse of these sloughs of ink!

The third morning, my copy was the first element of the *m* and *n*, or what in burlesque is called a hook. On my fourth, I had the last half of the same letters, or the trammel.

In this way I went through all the small letters, as they are called. First, the elements or constituent parts, then the whole character in which these parts were combined.

Then I must learn to make the capitals, before entering on joining hand. Four pages were devoted to these. Capital letters! They were capital offences against all that is graceful, indeed decent, yea tolerable, in that art which is so capable of beautiful forms and proportions.

I came next to joining hand, about three weeks after my commencement; and joining hand indeed it was! It seemed as if my hooks and trammels were overheated in the forge, and were melted into each other; the shapeless masses so clung together at points where they ought to have been separate, so very far were they from all resemblance to conjoined, yet distinct and well-defined characters.

Thus I went on, a perfect little prodigal in

the expenditure of paper, ink, pens, and time.
The first winter, I splashed two, and the next,
three writing-books with inky puddle, in learning coarse hand; and, after all, I had gained not
much in penmanship, except a workmanlike
assurance and celerity of execution, such as is
natural to an old hand at the business.

The third winter, I commenced small hand,
or rather fine, as it is more technically denomi-
nated; or rather a copy of half-way dimensions,
that the change to fine running-hand might not
be too sudden. From this dwarfish course, or
giant fine hand, — just as you please to call
it, — I slid down to the genuine epistolary and
mercantile, with a capital at the head of the
line, as much out of proportion as a corpulent
old captain marching in single file before a
parade of little boys.

Some of our teachers were accustomed to
spend a few minutes, forenoon and afternoon, in
going round among the writers to see that they
held the pen properly, and took a decent degree
of pains. But the majority of them, according to
present recollections, never stirred from the desk
to superintend this branch. There was something like an excuse, however, for not visiting
their pupils while at the pen. Sitting as they
did in those long, narrow, rickety seats, one

could hardly be got at without joggling two or three others, displacing a writing-book, knocking over an inkstand, and making a deal of rustle, rattle, and racket.

Some of the teachers set the copies at home in the evening, but most set them in school. Six hours per day were all that custom required of a teacher : of course, half an hour at home spent in the matters of the school would have been time and labor not paid for, and a gratuity not particularly expected. On entering in the morning, and looking for the master as the object at which to make the customary " manners," we could perceive just the crown of his head beyond a huge stack of manuscripts, which, together with his copy-setting attention, prevented the bowed and courtesied respects from his notice. A few of the most advanced in penmanship had copper-plate slips, as they were called, tucked into their manuscripts, for the trial of their more skillful hands ; or, if an ordinary learner had for once done extraordinarily well, he was permitted a slip as a mark of merit, and a circumstance of encouragement. Sometimes, when the master was pressed for time, all the joining-handers were thus furnished. It was a pleasure to have copies of this sort ; their polished shades, graceful curves, and deli-

cate hair lines, were so like a picture for the
eye to dwell upon.   But, when we set about
the work of imitation, discouragement took the
place of pleasure.   " After all, give us the
master's hand," we thought ; " we can come
up to that now and then."   We despaired of
ever becoming decent penmen with this copper-
plate perfection mocking our clumsy fingers.

There was one item in penmanship which
our teachers generally omitted altogether.   It
was the art of making and mending pens.   I
suffer, and others on my account suffer, from
this neglect even at this day.   The untraceable
" partridge tracks," as some one called them,
with which I perplex my correspondents, and
am now about to provoke the printer, are
chargeable to my ignorance in pen-making.   It
is a fact, however some acquaintances may
doubt it, that I generally write very legibly, if
not gracefully, whenever I borrow, beg, or
steal a pen.

Let not the faithful Wrifford, should his eye
chance to fall on this lament, think that I have
forgotten his twelve lessons, of one hour each,
on twelve successive, cold November days,
when I was just on the eve of commencing
pedagogue for the first time — (for I, too, have
kept a district school, in a manner somewhat

like " as it was ") — I have not forgotten them.
He did well for me. But, alas! his tall form
bent over my shoulder, his long flexile finger
adjusted my pen, and his vigilant eye glanced
his admonitions, in vain. That thirteenth
lesson which he added gratis, to teach us
pen-making, I was so unfortunate as to lose.
Lamentable to me and to many others, that I
was kept away.

I blush while I acknowledge it, but I have
taught school, have taught penmanship, have
made and mended a hundred pens a day, and
all the time I knew not much more of the art
of turning quill into pen, than did the goose
from whose wing it was plucked. But my
manufactures were received by my pupils, as
good. Good, of course, they must be; for the
master made them, and who should dare to
question *his* competency? If the instrument
did not operate well, the fault must certainly
be in the fingers that wielded, not those that
wrought it.

Chapter XIV

Seventh Winter, but not Much about it
— Eighth Winter — Mr. Johnson —
Good Order, and but Little Punish-
ing — a Story about Punishing —
Ninth Winter

OF my seventh winter I have but little to
say ; for but little was done worthy of
record here. We had an indolent master and
an idle school. Some tried to kindle up the
speaking spirit again ; but the teacher had no
taste that way. But there was dialoguing
enough nevertheless — in that form called *whispering*. Our school was a theater in earnest ;
for " plays " were going on all the time. It
was " acting " to the life, acting anyhow
rather than like scholars at their books. But
let that winter and its works, or rather want of
works, pass. Of the eighth I can say something worth notice, I think.

In consequence of the lax discipline of the
two last winters, the school had fallen into very
idle and turbulent habits. " A master that

will keep order, a master that will keep order!"
was the cry throughout the district. Accord-
ingly such a one was sought, and fortunately
found. A certain Mr. Johnson, who had
taught in a neighboring town, was famous for
his strictness, and that without much punishing.
He was obtained at a little higher price than
usual, and was thought to be well worth the
price. I will describe his person, and relate an
incident as characteristic of the man.

Mr. Johnson was full six feet high, with the
diameter of his chest and limbs in equal proportion. His face was long, and as dusky as a
Spaniard's; and the dark was still darkened by
the roots of an enormous beard. His eyes were
black, and looked floggings and blood from out
their cavernous sockets, which were overhung
by eyebrows not unlike brush-heaps. His hair
was black and curly, and extended down, and
expanded on each side of his face in a pair of
whiskers a freebooter might have envied.

He possessed the longest, widest, and thickest
ruler I ever saw. This was seldom brandished
in his hand, but generally lay in sight upon the
desk. Although he was so famous for his orders
in school, he scarcely ever had to use his puni-
tive instrument. His look, bearing, and voice
were enough for the subjection of the most riot-

ous school. Never was our school so still and
so studious as this winter. A circumstance occurred the very first day, which drove everything like mischief in consternation from every
scholar's heart. Abijah Wilkins had for years
been called the worst boy in school. Masters
could do nothing with him. He was surly, saucy,
profane, and truthless. Mr. Patch took him from
an alms-house when he was eight years old,
which was eight years before the point of time
now in view. In his family were mended
neither his disposition, his manners, nor even
his clothes. He looked like a morose, unpitied
pauper still. He had shaken his knurly and
filthy fist in the very face and eyes of the last
winter's teacher. Mr. Johnson was told of this
son of perdition before he began, and was prepared to take some efficient step at his first
offence.

Well, the afternoon of the first day, Abijah
thrust a pin into a boy beside him, which made
him suddenly cry out with the sharp pain. The
sufferer was questioned ; Abijah was accused,
and found guilty. The master requested James
Clark to go to his room, and bring a rattan he
would find there, as if the formidable ferule was
unequal to the present exigency. James came
with a rattan very long and very elastic, as if it

had been selected from a thousand, not to walk
with, but to whip. Then he ordered all the
blinds next to the road to be closed. He then
said, " Abijah, come this way." He came.
" The school may shut their books, and suspend
their studies a few minutes. Abijah, take off
your frock, fold it up, lay it on the seat behind
you." Abijah obeyed these several commands
with sullen tardiness. Here, a boy up towards
the back seat burst out with a sort of shuddering
laugh, produced by a nervous excitement he
could not control. " Silence ! " said the master,
with a thunder, and a stamp on the floor that
made the house quake. All was as still as midnight — not a foot moved, not a seat cracked,
not a book rustled. The school seemed to be
appalled. The expression of every countenance
was changed ; some were unnaturally pale, some
flushed, and eighty distended and moistened eyes
were fastened on the scene. The awful expectation was too much for one poor girl. " May
I go home ? " she whined with an imploring and
terrified look. A single glance from the countenance of authority crushed the trembler down
into her seat again. A tremulous sigh escaped
from one of the larger girls, then all was breath-
lessly still again. " Take off your jacket also,
Abijah. Fold it, and lay it on your frock."

Mr. Johnson then took his chair, and set it away at the farthest distance the floor would permit, as if all the space that could be had would be necessary for the operations about to take place. He then took the rattan, and seemed to examine it closely, drew it through his hand, bent it almost double, laid it down again. He then took off his own coat, folded it up, and laid it on the desk. Abijah's breast then heaved like a bellows, his limbs began to tremble, and his face was like a sheet. The master now took the rattan in his right hand, and the criminal by the collar with his left, his large knuckles pressing hard against the shoulder of the boy. He raised the stick high over the shrinking back. Then, oh! what a screech! Had the rod fallen? No, it still remained suspended in the air. "O — I won't do so agin — I'll *never* do so agin — O — O — don't — I will be good — sartinly will." The threatening instrument of pain was gently taken from its elevation. The master spoke: "You promise, do you?" "Yis, sir, — oh! yis, sir." The tight grasp was withdrawn from the collar. "Put on your frock and jacket, and go to your seat. The rest of you may now open your books." The school breathed again. Paper rustled, feet were carefully moved, the seats slightly cracked, and all

things went stilly on as before. Abijah kept
his promise. He became an altered boy; obe-
dient, peaceable, studious. This long and slow
process of preparing for the punishment was art-
fully designed by the master, gradually to work
up the boy's terrors and agonizing expectations
to the highest pitch, until he should yield like
a babe to the intensity of his emotions. His
stubborn nature, which had been like an oak
on the hills which no storm could prostrate, was
whittled away and demolished, as it were, sliver
by sliver.

Not Abijah Wilkins only, but the whole
school were subdued to the most humble and
habitual obedience by the scene I have described.
The terror of it seemed to abide in their hearts.
The school improved much this winter, that is,
according to the ideas of improvement then prevailing. Lessons were well gotten, and well
said, although the *why* and the *wherefore* of them
were not asked or given.

Mr. Johnson was employed the next winter
also, and it was the prevailing wish that he
should be engaged for the third time; but he
could not be obtained. His reputation as a
teacher had secured for him a school at twenty
dollars per month for the year round, in a distant village; so we were never more to sit " as

still as mice," in his most magisterial presence.
For years the saying in the district in respect to
him was, " He was the best master I ever went
to ; he kept such good order, and punished so
little."

Chapter XV

Going out — making Bows — Boys coming in — Girls going out and coming in

THE young are proverbially ignorant of the
value of time. There is one portion
of it, however, which they well know how to
appreciate. They feel it to be a wealth both
to body and soul. Its few moments are truly
golden ones, forming a glittering spot amid the
drossy dullness of in-school duration. I refer
to the forenoon and afternoon recess for " going
out." Consider that we came from all the
freedom of the farm, where we had the sweep
of acres — hills, valleys, woods, and waters,
and were crowded, I may say packed, into the
district box. Each one had scarcely more space
than would allow him to shift his head from an
inclination to one shoulder to an inclination to
the other, or from leaning on the right elbow,
to leaning on the left. There we were, the
blood of health bouncing through our veins,
feeding our strength, swelling our dimensions;

and there we must stay, three hours on a
stretch, with the exception of the aforementioned recess. No wonder that we should
prize this brief period high, and rush tumultu-
ously out doors to enjoy it.

There is one circumstance in going out which
so much amuses my recollection that I will
venture to describe it. It is the making of our
bows, or manners, as it is called. If one wishes
to see variety in the doing of a single act, let
him look at school-boys, leaving their bows at
the door. Tell me not of the diversities and
characteristics, of the gentilities and the awk-
wardnesses in the civility of shaking hands.
The bow is as diversified and characteristic, as
awkward or genteel, as any movement many-
motioned man is called on to make. Especially
in a country school, where fashion and polite-
ness have not altered the tendencies of nature
by forming the manners of all after one model
of propriety. Besides, the bow was before the
shake, both in the history of the world, and in
that of every individual man. No doubt the
world's first gentleman, nature-taught, declined
his head in some sort, in saluting for the first
time the world's first lady, in primitive Eden.
And no doubt every little boy has been instructed to make a " nice bow," from chubby

Cain, Abel, and Seth, down to the mannered younglings of the present day.

Well, then, it is near half-past ten, A.M., but seemingly eleven to the impatient youngsters; anticipation rather than reflection, being the faculty most in action just now. At last the master takes out his watch, and gives a hasty glance at the index of the hour. Or, if this premonitory symptom does not appear, watching eyes can discern the signs of the time in the face relaxing itself from severe duty, and in the moving lips just assuming that precise form necessary to pronounce the sentence of liberation. Then, make ready, take aim, is at once the order of every idler. "The boys may go out." The little white heads on the little seat, as it is called, are the foremost, having nothing in front to impede a straight-forward sally. One little nimble-foot is at the door in an instant; and, as he lifts the latch, he tosses off a bow over his left shoulder, and is out in a twinkling. The next perhaps squares himself towards the master with more precision, not having his attention divided between opening the door and leaving his manners. Next comes the very least of the little, just in front of the big-boy rush behind him, tap-tapping and tottering along the floor, with his finger in his nose; but, in wheeling from his bow, he blunders head first through the door, in his anxiety to get out of the way of the impending throng of fists and knees behind, in avoiding which he is prostrated under the tramp of cowhide.

Now come the Bigs from behind the writing benches. Some of them make a bow with a jerk of the head and snap of the neck possible only to giddy-brained, oily-jointed boyhood. Some, whose mothers are of the precise cast, or who have had their manners stiffened at a dancing-school, will wait till the throng is a little thinned; and then they will strut out with their arms as straight at their sides as if there were no such things as elbows, and will let their upper person bend upon the middle hinge, as if this were the only joint in their frames. Some look straight at their toes, as the face descends toward the floor. Others strain a glance up at the master, displaying an uncommon proportion of that beauty of the eye, — the white. Lastly come the tenants of the extreme back seat, the Anaks of the school. One long-limbed, lank-sided, back-bending fellow of twenty is at the door at four strides; he has the proper curve already prepared by his ordinary gait, and he has nothing to do but swing round towards the master, and his manners are made. Another, whose

H

body is developed in the full proportions of manhood, turns himself half way, and just gives the slightest inclination of the person. He thinks himself too much of a man to make such a ridiculous popping of the pate as the younglings who have preceded him. Another, with a tread that makes the floor tremble, goes straight out through the open door, without turning to the right or left; as much as to say, "I am quite too old for that business."

There are two in the short seat at the end of the spelling-floor who have almost attained to the glorious, or rather vain-glorious age of twenty-one. They are perhaps even more aged than the venerable Rabbi of the school himself. So they respect their years, and put away childish things, inasmuch as they do not go out as their juniors do. One of them sticks to his slate. It is his last winter; and, as he did not catch flying time by the forelock, he must cling to his heel. The other unpuckers his arithmetical brow, puts his pencil between his teeth, leans his head on his right palm, with his left fingers adjusts his foretop, and then composes himself into an amiable gaze upon the fair remainder of the school. Perhaps his eyes leap at once to that damsel of eighteen in the furthermost seat, who is the secret mistress of his heart.

How still it is in the absence of half the limbs and lips of the domain! That little girl who has been buzzing round her lesson like a bee round a honey-suckle, off and on by turns, is now sipping its sweets, if any sweets there be, as closely and stilly as that same bee plunged in the bell of the flower. The secret of the unwonted silence is, the master knows on which side of the aisle to look for noise and mischief now.

It is time for the boys to come in. The master raps on the window as a signal. At first they scatter in one by one, keeping the door on the slam, slam. But soon, in rush the main body, pell-mell, rubbing their ears, kicking their heels, puffing, panting, wheezing. Impelled by the temporary chill, they crowd round the fire, regaining the needed warmth as much by the exercise of elbows as by the heat of fuel. "Take your seats, you that have got warm," says the master. No one starts. "Take your seats, all of you." Tramp, tramp, how the floor trembles again, and the seats clatter. There goes an inkstand. Ben pinches Tom to let him know that he must go in first. Tom stands back; but gives Ben a kick on the shins as he passes, to pay for that pinch.

"The girls may go out." The noise and

confusion are now of the feminine gender. Trip, trip, rustle, rustle. Shall I describe the diversities of the courtesy? I could pen a trait or two, but prefer to leave the subject to the more discriminating quill of the courtesying sex. The shrill tones and gossiping chatter of girlhood now ring from without. But they do not stay long. Trip, trip, rustle, rustle back again. Half of them are sucking a lump of snow for drink. One has broken an icicle from the well-spout, and is nibbing it as she would a stick of candy. See Sarah jump. The ice-eater's cold, dripping hand has mischievously sprinkled her neck. Down goes the melting little cone, and is scattered in shivers. "Take your seats," says authority with soft command. He is immediately obeyed; and the dull routine rolls on toward noon.

Chapter XVI

Noon — Noise and Dinner — Sports at
School — Coasting — Snow-balling — a
Certain Memorable Snow-ball Battle

NOON has come. It is even half-past
twelve; for the teacher got puzzled with
a hard sum, and did not attend to the second
reading of the first class so soon as usual by
half an hour. It has been hitch, hitch — joggle,
joggle — creak, creak, all over the school-room
for a considerable time. " You are dismissed,"
comes at last. The going out of half the
school only was a noisy business; but now
there is a tenfold thunder, augmented by the
windy rush of many petticoats. All the voices
of all the tongues now split or rather shatter
the air, if I may so speak. There are more
various tones than could be indicated by all the
epithets ever applied to sound.

The first manual operation is the extracting
of certain parcels from pockets, bags, baskets,
hat-crowns, and perhaps the capacious cavity
formed by the tie of a short open frock. Then

what a savory development, — bread, cheese, cakes, pies, sausages, and apples without number! It is voice *versus* appetite now for the occupancy of the mouth.

The case is soon decided, that is, dinner is dispatched. Then commences what, in view of most of us, is the chief business of the day. Before describing this, however, I would premise a little. The principal allurement and prime happiness of going to school, as it used to be conducted, was the opportunity it afforded for social amusement. Our rural abodes were scattered generally a half or a quarter of a mile apart, and the young could not see each other every day as conveniently as they can in a city or a village. The schooling season was therefore looked forward to as one long series of holidays, or, as Mark Martin once said, as so many thanksgiving days, except the music, the sermon, and the dinner. Mark Martin, let me mention by the way, was the wit of the school. Some of his sayings, that made us laugh at the time, I shall hereafter put down. They may not affect the reader, however, as they did us, for the lack of his peculiar manner which set them off.

Of all the sportive exercises of the winter school, the most exhilarating, indeed intensely delightful, was sliding down hill, or coasting, as it is called. The location of our school was uncommonly favorable for this diversion. Situated as we were on a hill, we could go down like arrows for the eighth of a mile on one side, and half that distance on the other. Almost every boy had his sled. Some of us got our names branded on the vehicle, and prided ourselves in the workmanship or the swiftness of it, as mariners do in that of a ship. We used to personify the dear little speeder with a she and a her, seamanlike also. Take it when a few days of severely cold and clear weather have permitted the road to be worn icy smooth, and the careering little coaster is the most enviable pleasure-rider that was ever eager to set out or sorry to stop. The very tugging up hill back again, is not without its pleasure. The change of posture is agreeable, and also the stir of limb and stretch of muscle for the short time required to return to the starting place. Then there is the looking forward to the glorious down hill again. In all the pleasures of human experience, there is nothing like coasting, for the regular alternation of glowing anticipation and frame-thrilling enjoyment.

Another sport which comes only with the winter, and is enjoyed mostly at school is the chivalrous pastime of snow-balling. Take, for instance, the earliest snow of winter, falling gently and stilly with its feathery flakes, of just the right moisture for easy manipulation. Or when the drifts soften in the mid-winter thaw, or begin to settle beneath the lengthened and sunny days of March, then is the season for the power and glory of a snow-ball fight. The whole school of the martial sex are out of a noon-time, from the veterans of a hundred battles down almost to the freshest recruits of the little front seat. Half against half, unless a certain number agree to " take " all the rest. The oldest are opposed to the oldest in the hostile array, so that the little round, and perhaps hard, missile may not be out of proportion to the age, size, and toughness of the antagonist likely to be hit. The little boys, of course, against the little, with this advantage, that their discharges lose most of their force before reaching the object aimed at. When one is hit, he is not merely wounded; he is a dead man as to this battle. Here, no quarter is asked or given. The balls whistle, the men fall, until all are defunct but one or two individuals, who remain unkilled because there is no enemy left to hurl the fatal ball.

But our conflicts were not always make-

believes, and conducted according to the formal
rules of play: these sham-fights sometimes
waxed into the very reality of war.

The school was about equally divided between
the East and the West ends of the district.
From time immemorial there had come down
a rivalry between the two parties in respect to
physical activity and strength. At the close of
the school in the afternoon, and at the parting
of the scholars on their different ways toward
home, there were almost always a few farewells
in the form of a sudden trip-up, a dab of snow,
or an icy-ball almost as tenderly soft and agreeable of contact as that mellow thing—a stone.
These valedictories were as courteously recipro-
cated from the other side.

These slight skirmishes would sometimes
grow into a general battle, when the arm was
not careful to proportion the force just so as to
touch and no more, as in a noon-day game.

One battle I recollect, which is worthy of
being commemorated in a book, at least a book
about boyhood, like this. It is as fresh before
my mind's eye as if it were but yesterday.

It had gently but steadily snowed all one
December night, and almost all the next day.
Owing to the weather, there were no girls ex-
cepting Capt. Clark's two, and no very small

boys, at school. The scholars had been unusually playful through the day, and had taken liberties which would not have been tolerated in the full school.

When we were dismissed at night, the snow had done falling, and the ammunition of just the right moisture lay in exhaustless abundance on the ground, all as level as a floor; for there had been no wind to distribute unequally the gifts of the impartial clouds. The first boy that sprang from the threshold caught up a quart of the spotless but viscid material, and whitewashed the face of the next one at the door, who happened to belong to the rival side. This was a signal for general action. As fast as the troops poured out, they rushed to the conflict. We had not the coolness deliberately to arrange ourselves in battle-order, line against line; but each aimed at each as he could, no matter whom, how, or where, provided that he belonged to the "other End." We did not round the snow into shape, but hurled and dashed it in large masses, as we happened to snatch or scoop it up. As the combatants in gunpowder war are hidden from each other by clouds of their own raising, so also our warriors clouded themselves from sight. And there were other obstacles to vision besides the discharges in the air; for one, or both of the eyes of us all were glued up and sealed in darkness by the damp, sticky matter. The nasal and auditory cavities too were temporarily closed. And here and there a mouth, opening after a little breath, received the same snowy visitation.

At length, from putting snow into each other, we took to putting each other into the snow. Not by the formal and deliberate wrestle, but pell-mell, hurly-burly, as foot, hand, or head could find an advantage. The combatants were covered with the clinging element. It was as if their woolen habiliments had turned back to their original white. So completely were we all besmeared by the same material, that we could not tell friend from foe in the blind encounter. No matter for this; we were now crazed with fun; and we were ready to carry it to the utmost extent that time and space and snow would admit. Just opposite the school-house door, the hill descended very steeply from the road for about ren rods. The stone wall just here was quite low, and completely covered with snow even before this last fall. The two stoutest champions of the fray had been snowing it into each other like storm-spirits from the two opposite poles. At length, as if their snow-bolts were exhausted, they seized each other for the tug of muscle with muscle. They had unconsciously worked themselves to the precipitous brink. Another stout fellow caught a glimpse of their position, gave a rush and a push, and both Arctic and Antarctic went tumbling heels hindmost down the steep declivity, until they were stopped by the new-fallen snow in which they were completely buried; and one with his nose downward as if he had voluntarily dived into his own grave. This was a signal for a general push-off, and the performer of the sudden exploit was the first to be gathered to his victims below. In five minutes, all were in the same predicament but one, who, not finding himself attacked, wiped the plaster from his eyes, and saw himself the lone hero of the field. He gave a victorious shout; then, not liking solitude for a playmate, he made a dauntless leap after the rest, who were now thickly rising from their snowy burial to life, action, and fun anew. Now the game is to put each other down, down, to the bottom of the hill. There is pulling, pushing, pitching, and whirling, every species of manual attack, except the pugilistic thump and knock-down. One long lubber has fallen exactly parallel with the bottom; and, before he can recover himself, two others are rolling him down like a senseless log, until the

lumberers themselves are pitched head first over
their timber by other hands still behind them.
But at length we are all at the bottom of the
hill, and indeed at the bottom of our strength.
Which End, the East or the West, had the day,
could not be determined. In one sense it belonged to neither, for it was night. We now
found ourselves in a plight not particularly comfortable to ourselves, nor likely to be very agreeable to the domestic guardians we must now
meet. But the battle has been described, and
that is enough: there is no glory in the suffering that succeeds.

Chapter XVII

Arithmetic — Commencement — Progress — Late Improvement in the Art of Teaching

AT the age of twelve, I commenced the study of Arithmetic, that chiefest of sciences in Yankee estimation. No man is willing that his son should be without skill in figures. And if he does not teach him his A B C at home, he will the art of counting, at least. Many a father deems it no hardship to instruct his child to enumerate even up to a hundred, when it would seem beyond his capacity, or certainly beyond the leisure of his rainy days and winter evenings, to sit down with the formality of a book, and teach him to read.

The entering on arithmetic was quite an era in my school-boy life. This was placing me decidedly among the great boys, and within hailing distance of manhood. My feelings were consequently considerably elevated. A new Adams's Arithmetic of the latest edition was bought for my use. It was covered by the maternal hand with stout sheepskin, in the economical expectation, that, after I had done with it, it might help still younger heads to the golden science. A quire of foolscap was made to take the form of a manuscript of the full length of the sheet, with a pasteboard cover, as more suitable to the dignity of such superior dimensions than flimsy brown paper.

I had also a bran new slate, for Ben used father's old one. It was set in a frame wrought by the aforesaid Ben, who prided himself on his knack at tools, considering that he had never served an apprenticeship at their use. There was no lack of timber in the fabrication. Mark Martin said that he could make a better frame with a jack-knife in his left hand, and keep his right in his pocket.

My first exercise was transcribing from my Arithmetic to my manuscript. At the top of the first page I penned ARITHMETIC, in capitals an inch high, and so broad that this one word reached entirely across the page. At a due distance below, I wrote the word ADDITION in large, coarse hand, beginning with a lofty A, which seemed like the drawing of a mountain peak, towering above the level wilderness below. Then came *Rule*, in a little smaller hand, so that there was a regular gradation from the enormous capitals at the top, down to the fine running — no, hobbling hand in which I wrote off the rule.

Now slate and pencil and brain came into use. I met with no difficulty at first; Simple Addition was as easy as counting my fingers. But there was one thing I could not understand —that carrying of tens. It was absolutely necessary, I perceived, in order to get the right answer; yet it was a mystery which that arithmetical oracle, our schoolmaster, did not see fit to explain. It is possible that it was a mystery to him. Then came Subtraction. The borrowing of ten was another unaccountable operation. The reason seemed to me then at the very bottom of the well of science; and there it remained for that winter, for no friendly bucket brought it up to my reach.

Every rule was transcribed to my manuscript, and each sum likewise as it stood proposed in the book, and also the whole process of figures by which the answer was found.

Each rule, moreover, was, or rather was to be, committed to memory, word for word, which to me was the most tedious and difficult job of the whole.

I advanced as far as Reduction this first winter, and a third through my manuscript, perhaps. The end of the Arithmetic seemed almost as far off in the future as that end of boyhood and under-age restraint, twenty-one.

The next winter I began at Addition again, to advance just through Interest. My third season I went over the same ground again, and, besides that, ciphered to the very last sum in the Rule of Three. This was deemed quite an achievement for a lad only fourteen years old, according to the ideas prevailing at that period. Indeed, whoever ciphered through the above-mentioned rule was supposed to have arithmetic enough for the common purposes of life. If one proceeded a few rules beyond this, he was considered quite smart. But if he went clear through — Miscellaneous Questions and all — he was thought to have an extraordinary taste and genius for figures. Now and then, a youth, after having been through Adams, entered upon old Pike, the arithmetical sage who "set the sums" for the preceding generation. Such were called great "arithmeticians."

The fourth winter I advanced — but it is not important to the purpose of this work that I should record the minutiæ of my progress in the science of numbers. Suffice it to say, that I was not one of the "great at figures."

I

The female portion of the school, we may suppose, generally expected to obtain husbands to perform whatever arithmetical operations they might need, beyond the counting of fingers : so the science found no special favor with them. If pursued at all, it was neglected till the last year or two of their schooling. Most were provident enough to cipher as far as through the four simple rules; for although they had no idea of becoming old maids, they might possibly, however, be left widows. Had arithmetic been pursued at the summer school, those who intended to be summer teachers would probably have thought more of the science, and have proceeded further, even perhaps to the Rule of Three. But a schoolmistress would as soon have expected to teach the Arabic language as the numerical science. So, ignorance of it was no dishonor even to the first and best of the sex.

Chapter XVIII

Augustus Starr, the Privateer who turned Pedagogue — his New Crew mutiny, and perform a Singular Exploit

MY tenth winter, our school was put under the instruction of a person named Augustus Starr. He was a native of a neighboring town, and was acquainted with the committee. He had taught school some years before, but of late had been engaged in a business not particularly conducive to improvement in the art of teaching. He had been an inferior officer aboard a privateer in the late war, which terminated the previous winter. At the return of peace, he betook himself to land; and, till something more suitable to his tastes and habits should offer, he concluded to resume school-keeping, at least for one winter.

He came to our town; and, finding an old acquaintance seeking for a teacher, he offered himself, and was accepted. He was rather genteelly dressed, and gentlemanly in his manners.

Mr. Starr soon manifested that stern command, rather than mild persuasion, had been his method of preserving order, and was to be, still. This would have been put up with; but he soon showed that he could deal in blows as well as words, and these not merely with the customary ferule, or supple and tingling stick, but with whatever came to hand. He knocked one lad down with his fist, hurled a stick of wood at another, which missed breaking his head because it struck the ceiling, making a dent which fearfully indicated what would have been the consequence had the skull been hit. The scholars were terrified, parents were alarmed, and some kept their younger children at home. There was an uproar in the district. A school-meeting was threatened for the purpose of dismissing the captain, as he began to be called, in reference to the station he had lately filled, although it was not a captaincy. But he commanded the school-house crew: so, in speaking of him, they gave him a corresponding title. In consequence of these indications, our officer became less dangerous in his modes of punishment, and was permitted to continue still in command. But he was terribly severe, nevertheless; and in his words of menace, he mani-

fested no particular respect for that one of the
ten commandments which forbids profanity.
But he took pains with his pupils, and they
made considerable progress according to the
prevailing notions of education.

Toward the close of the school, however,
Starr's fractious temper, his cuffs, thumps, and
cudgelings, waxed dangerous again.   There
were signs of mutiny among the large scholars,
and there were provocations and loud talk
among parents.   The man of violence, even at
this late period, would have been dismissed by
the authority of the district, had not a sudden
and less formal ejection overtaken him.

The captain had been outrageously severe,
and even cruel, to some of the smaller boys.
The older brothers of the sufferers, with others
of the back seat, declared among themselves,
that they would put him by force out of the
school-house, if anything of the like should
happen again.   The very afternoon succeeding
this resolution, an opportunity offered to put it
to the test.   John Howe, for some trifling misdemeanor, received a cut with the edge of the
ruler on his head, which drew blood.   The
dripping wound and the scream of the boy
were a signal for action, as if a murderer were
at his fell deed before their eyes.   Thomas

Howe, one of the oldest in the school and the brother of the abused, and Mark Martin, were at the side of our privateer in an instant. Two others followed. His ruler was wrested from his hand, and he was seized by his legs and shoulders, before he could scarcely think into what hands he had fallen. He was carried, kicking and swearing, out of doors. But this was not the end of his headlong and horizontal career. "To the side hill, to the side hill," cried Mark, who had him by the head. Now it so happened that the hillside opposite the school-house door was crusted, and as smooth and slippery as pure ice, from a recent rain. To this pitch, then, he was borne, and in all the haste that his violent struggles would permit. Over he was thrust, as if he were a log; and down he went, giving one of his bearers a kick as he was shoved from their hands, which action of the foot sent him more swiftly on his way from the rebound. There was no bush or stone to catch by in his descent, and he clawed the unyielding crust with his nails, for the want of anything more prominent on which to lay hold. Down, down he went. Oh for a pile of stones or a thicket of thorns to cling to, even at the expense of torn apparel or scratched fingers! Down, down he went, until he fairly came to the climax, or rather anti-climax, of his pedagogical career.

When our master had come to a " period or full stop," to quote from the spelling-book, he lay a moment as if he had left his breath behind him, or as if querying whether he should consider himself alive or not; or perhaps whether it were really his own honorable self who had been voyaging in this unseamanlike fashion, or somebody else. He at length arose and stood upright, facing the ship of literature which he had lately commanded; and his mutinous crew, great and small, male and female, now lining the side of the road next to the declivity, from which most of them had witnessed his expedition. The movement had been so sudden, and the ejection so unanticipated by the school in general, that they were stupefied with amazement. And the bold performers of the exploit were almost as much amazed as the rest, excepting Mark, who still retained coolness enough for his joke. " What think of the *coasting* trade, captain ? " shouted Mark; " is it as profitable as privateering ? " Our coaster made no reply, but turned in pursuit of a convenient footing to get up into the road, and to the school-house again. While he was at a distance approaching his late station

of command, Mark Martin stepped forward to
hold a parley with him. "We have a word to
say to you, sir, before you come much farther.
If you will come back peaceably, you may
come; but as sure as you meddle with any of
us, we will make you acquainted with the *heft*
and the hardness of our fists, and of stones and
clubs too, if we must. The ship is no longer
yours; so look out, for we are our own men
now." Starr replied, "I do not wish to have
anything more to do with the school; but
there is another law besides club law, and that
you have got to take." But when he came up
and saw John Howe's face stained with blood,
and his head bound up as if it had received the
stroke of a cutlass, he began to look rather
blank. Our spokesman reminded him of what
he had done, and inquired, "which is the
worse, a ride and a slide, or a gashed head?"
"I rather guess that you are the one to look
out for the law," said Thomas Howe, with a
threatening tone and look. Whether this hint
had effect, I know not, but he never commenced a prosecution. He gathered up his
goods and chattels, and left the school-house.
The scholars gathered up their implements of
learning, and left likewise, after the boys had
taken one more glorious slide down hill.

There were both gladness and regret in that
dispersion;—gladness that they had no more
broken heads, shattered hands, and skinned
backs to fear; and regret that the season of
schooling, and of social and delightful play, had
been cut short by a week.

The news reached most of the district in the
course of the next day, that our " man of war,"
as he was sometimes called, had sailed out of
port the night before.

Chapter XIX

Eleventh Winter — Mr. Silverson, our
First Teacher from College — his Blun-
der at Meeting on the Sabbath — his
Character as a Schoolmaster

THIS winter, Major Allen was the committee; and, of course, everybody expected
a dear master, if not a good one; he had always
expressed himself so decidedly against " your
cheap trash." They were not disappointed.
They had a dear master, high priced and not
much worth. Major Allen sent to college for
an instructor, as a young gentleman from such
an institution must of course be qualified as to
learning, and would give a higher tone to the
school. He had good reason for the expectation, as a gentleman from the same institution
had taught the two preceding winters in
another town where Major Allen was inti-
mately acquainted, and gave the highest satisfaction. But he was a very different sort of
person from Mr. Frederic Silverson, of the city
of ——, member of the junior class in ——

College. This young gentleman did not teach eight weeks, at eighteen dollars per month, for the sake of the trifling sum to pay his college bills, and help him to rub a little more easily through. He kept for fun, as he told his fellow bucks; that is, to see the fashions of country life, to "cut capers" among folks whose opinion he didn't care for, and to bring back something to laugh about all the next term. The money, too, was a consideration, as it would pay a bill or two which he preferred that his very indulgent father should not know of.

Major Allen had written to some of the college authorities for an instructor, not doubting that he should obtain one of proved worth, or at least one who had been acquainted with country schools in his boyhood, and would undertake with such motives as would insure a faithful discharge of his duties. But a tutor, an intimate acquaintance of Silverson's family, was requested to aid the self-rusticating son to a school; so by this means this city beau and college buck was sent to preside over our district seminary of letters.

Well, Mr. Silverson arrived on Saturday evening at Capt. Clark's. Sunday, he went to meeting. He was, indeed, a very genteel-looking personage, and caused quite a sensation among the young people in our meeting-house, especially those of our district. He was tall, but rather slender, with a delicate skin, and a cheek whose roses had not been uprooted from their native bed by what, in college, is called hard digging. His hair was cut and combed in the newest fashion, as was supposed, being arranged very differently from that of our young men. Then he wore a cloak of many-colored plaid, in which flaming red, however, was predominant. A plaid cloak — this was a new thing in our obscure town at that period, and struck us with admiration. We had seen nothing but surtouts and greatcoats from our fathers' sheep and our mothers' looms. His cravat was tied behind; this was another novelty. We had never dreamed but that the knot should be made, and the ends should dangle beneath the chin. Then his bosom flourished with a ruffle, and glistened with a breast-pin, such as were seldom seen so far among the hills.

Capt. Clark unconsciously assumed a stateliness of gait unusual to him, as he led the way up the center aisle, introduced the gentleman into his pew, and gave him his own seat, that is, next the isle, and the most respectable in the pew. The young gentleman, not having been accustomed to such deference in public, was a

little confused; and when he heard, " That is
the new master," whispered very distinctly by
some one near, and, on looking up, saw himself
the center of an all-surrounding stare, he was
smitten with a fit of bashfulness, such as he had
never felt before. So he quiddled with his fingers, sucked and bit his lips, as a relief to his
feelings, the same as those rustic starers would
have done at a splendid party in his mother's
drawing-rooms. During singing, he was intent
on the hymn-book, in the prayer he bent over
the pew-side, and during the sermon looked
straight at the preacher — a churchlike deport-
ment which he had never, perhaps, manifested
before, and probably may never have since. He
was certainly not so severely decorous in that
meeting-house again. After the forenoon services, he committed a most egregious blunder,
by which his bashfulness was swallowed up in
shame. It was the custom in country towns
then, for all who sat upon the center or broad
aisle, as it was called, to remain in their pews
till the reverend man of the pulpit had passed
along by. Our city-bred gentleman was not
apprised of this etiquette; for it did not prevail
in the metropolis. Well, as soon as the last
amen was pronounced, Capt. Clark politely
handed him his hat; and, being next to the pew

door, he supposed he must make his egress first. He stepped out, and had gone several feet down the aisle, when he observed old and young standing in their pews on both sides, in front of his advance, staring at him as if surprised, and some of them with an incipient laugh. He turned his head, and gave a glance back; and, behold, he was alone in the long avenue, with a double line of eyes aimed at him from behind as well as before. All seemed waiting for the minister, who by this time had just reached the foot of the pulpit stairs. He was confounded with a consciousness of his mistake. Should he keep on or return to the pew, was a momentary question. It was a dilemma worse than any in logic. But finally, back he was going, when, behold, Capt. Clark's pew was blocked up by the out-poured and out-pouring throng of people, with the minister at their head. What should he do now? He wheeled again, dropped his head, put his left hand to his face, and went crouching down the aisle, and out of the door, like a boy going out with the nose-bleed.

On the ensuing morning, our collegian commenced school. He had never taught, and had never resided in the country before. He had acquired a knowledge of the daily routine usually pursued in school, from a class-mate who

had some experience in the vocation; so he
began things right end foremost, and finished at
the other extremity in due order; but they were
most clumsily handled all the way through.
His first fault was exceeding indolence. He
had escaped beyond the call of the morning
prayer-bell, that had roused him at dawn, and
he seemed resolved to replenish his nature with
sleep. He was generally awakened to the consciousness of being a schoolmaster by the ringing
shouts of his waiting pupils. Then a country
breakfast was too delicious a contrast to college
commons to be cut short. Thus that point of
duration called nine o'clock, and school time,
often approximated exceedingly near to ten that
winter.

Mr. Silverson did not visit in the several
families of the district, as most of his predecessors had done. He would have been pleased to
visit at every house, for he was socially inclined;
and what was more, he desired to pick up "food
for fun" when he should return to college.
But the people did not think themselves "smart"
enough to entertain a collegian, and the son of
the rich Mr. ——, of the city of ——, besides.
Or, perhaps, what is coming nearer the precise
truth, his habits and pursuits were so different
from theirs, that they did not know exactly how

to get at him, and in what manner to attempt
to entertain him; and he, on the other hand, did
not know how to fall into the train of their associations in his conversation, so as to make them
feel at ease, and, as it were, at home with him.
Another circumstance ought to be mentioned,
perhaps. The people very soon contracted a
growing prejudice against our schoolmaster, on
account of his very evident unfitness for his
present vocation, and especially his unpardon-
able indolence and neglect of duty.

So Mr. Silverson was not invited out, excepting by Major Allen, who engaged him, and by
two or three others who chanced to come in
contact with him, and to find him more sociably
disposed, and a less formidable personage, than
they anticipated. He spent most of his evenings, therefore, at his boarding-place, with one
volume in his hand, generally that of a novel,
and another volume issuing from his mouth, —
that of smoke; and as his chief object was just
to kill time, he was not careful that the former
should not be as fumy, as baseless, and as un-
profitable as the latter. As for the Greek,
Latin, and mathematics, to which he should
have devoted some portion of his time, according to the college regulations, he never looked
at them till his return. Then he just glanced

them over, and trusted luck when he was examined for two weeks' study, as he had done a hundred times before at his daily recitation.

What our young college buck carried back to laugh about all the next term, I do not know, unless it was his own dear self, for being so foolish as to undertake a business for which he was so utterly unfit, and from which he derived so little pleasure, compared with his anticipations.

K

Chapter XX

A College Master again—his Character
in School and out — our First Attempts at Composition — Brief Sketch
of Another Teacher

MY twelfth winter has arrived. It was
thought best to try a teacher from college again, as the committee had been assured
that there were teachers to be found there of
the first order, and well worth the high price
they demanded for their services. A Mr. Ellis
was engaged at twenty dollars per month, from
the same institution mentioned before. Particular pains were taken to ascertain the college
character, and the school-keeping experience of
the gentleman, before his engagement, and they
were such as to warrant the highest expectations.

The instructor was to board round in the
several families of the district, who gave
the board an order to lengthen the school
to the usual term. It happened that he was
to be at our house the first week. On Satur-

day Mr. Ellis arrived. It was a great event to
us children for the master to stop at our house,
and one from college too. We were smitten
with bashfulness, and stiffened into an awkwardness unusual with us, even among strangers.
But this did not last long. Our guest put us
all at ease very soon. He seemed just like one
of us, or like some unpuffed-up uncle from gen-
teeler life, who had dropped in upon us for a
night, with cordial heart, chatty tongue, and
merry laugh. He seemed perfectly acquainted
with our prevailing thoughts and feelings, and
let his conversation slide into the current they
flowed in, as easily as if he had never been
nearer college than we ourselves. With my
father he talked about the price of produce, the
various processes and improvements in agri-
culture, and the politics of the day, and such
other topics as would be likely to interest a
farmer so far in the country. And those
topics, indeed, were not a few. Some students
would have sat in dignified or rather dumpish
silence, and have gone to bed by mid-evening,
simply because those who sat with them could
not discourse on those deep things of science,
and lofty matters of literature, which were particularly interesting to themselves. With my
mother Mr. Ellis talked at first about her

children. He patted a little brother on his cheek, took a sister on his knee, and inquired the baby's name. Then he drew forth a housewifely strain concerning various matters in country domestic life. Of me he inquired respecting my studies at school years past; and even condescended to speak of his own boyhood and youth, and of the sports as well as the duties of school. The fact is, that Mr. Ellis had always lived in the country till three years past; his mind was full of rural remembrances; and he knew just how to take us to be agreeable himself, and to elicit entertainment in return.

Mr. Ellis showed himself at home in school, as well as at the domestic fireside. He was perfectly familiar with his duties, as custom had prescribed them, but he did not abide altogether by the old usages. He spent much time in explaining those rules in arithmetic and grammar, and those passages in the spelling-book, with which we had hitherto lumbered our memories.

This teacher introduced a new exercise into our school, that we had never thought of before as being possible to ourselves. It was composition. We hardly knew what to make of it. To write — to put sentence after sentence like a newspaper, a book, or a sermon — oh! we could not do this; we could not think of such a thing; indeed, it was an impossibility. But we must try, at any rate. The subject given out for this novel use of thought and pen was friendship. Friendship — what had we to say on this subject? We could feel on it, perhaps, especially those of us who had read a novel or two, and had dreamed of eternal friendship. But we had not a single idea. Friendship! oh! it is a delightful thing! This, or something similar, was about all we poor creatures could think of. What a spectacle of wretchedness did we present! A stranger would have supposed us all smitten with the toothache, by the agony expressed in the face. One poor girl put her head down into a corner, and cried till the master excused her. And, finally, finding that neither smiles nor frowns would put ideas into our heads, he let us go for that week.

In about a fortnight, to our horror, the exercise was proposed again. But it was only to write a letter. Any one could do as much as this, the master said; for almost every one had occasion to do it in the course of life. Indeed, we thought, on the whole, that we *could* write a letter, so at it we went with considerable alacrity.

But our attempts at the epistolary were nothing like those spirited, and even witty, products of thought which used ever to be flying from seat to seat in the shape of billets. The sprightly fancy and the gushing heart seemed to have been chilled and deadened by the reflection that a letter *must* be written, and the master *must* see it. These epistolary compositions generally began, continued, and closed all in the same way, as if all had got the same receipt from their grandmothers for letter writing. They mostly commenced in this manner: "Dear friend, I take my pen in hand to inform you that I am well, and hope you are enjoying the same blessing." Then there would be added, perhaps, "We have a very good schoolmaster; have you a good one? How long has your school got to keep? We have had a terribly stormy time on't," &c. Mark Martin addressed the master in his epistle. What its contents were I could not find out; but I saw Mr. Ellis read it. At first he looked grave, as at the assurance of the youth; then a little severe, as if his dignity was outraged; but in a moment he smiled, and finally he almost burst out with laughter at some closing witticism.

Mark's was the only composition that had any nature and soul in it. He wrote what he

thought, instead of thinking what to write, like
the rest of us, who, in the effort, thought just
nothing at all; for we wrote words which we
had seen written a hundred times before.

Mr. Ellis succeeded in delivering us from our
stale and flat formalities before he had done.
He gave us no more such abstract and lack-idea
subjects as friendship. He learned better how
to accommodate the theme to the youthful mind.
We were set to describe what we had seen with
our eyes, heard with our ears, and what had
particularly interested our feelings at one time
and another. One boy described the process
of cider-making. Another gave an account of a
squirrel-hunt; another of a great husking; each
of which had been witnessed the autumn before.
The girls described certain domestic operations.
One, I remember, gave quite an amusing account
of the coming and going, and final tarrying, of
her mother's soap. Another penned a sprightly
dialogue, supposed to have taken place between
two sisters on the question, which should go a
visiting with mother, and which should stay at
home and " take care of the things."

The second winter (for he taught two), Mr.
Ellis occasionally proposed more abstract subjects, and such as required more thinking and
reasoning, but still, such as were likely to be

interesting, and on which he knew his scholars to possess at least a few ideas.

I need not say how popular Mr. Ellis was in the district. He was decidedly the best schoolmaster I ever went to, and he was the last.

I have given him a place here, not because he is to be classed with his predecessors who taught the district school as it *was*, but because he closed the series of my own instructors there, and was the last, moreover, who occupied the old school-house. He commenced a new era in our district.

Before closing, I must give one necessary hint. Let it not be inferred from this narrative of my own particular experience, that the best teachers of district schools are to be found in college only. The very next winter, the school was blessed with an instructor even superior to Mr. Ellis, although he was not a collegian. Mr. Henry, however, had well disciplined and informed his mind, and was, moreover, an experienced teacher. I was not one of his pupils; but I was in the neighborhood, and knew of his methods, his faithfulness, and success. His tall, spare, stooping, and dyspeptic form is now distinctly before my mind's eye. I see him wearied with incessant exertion, taking his way homeward at the close of the afternoon school. His pockets are filled with compositions, to be looked over in private. There are school-papers in his hat too. A large bundle of writing-books is under his arm. Through the long evening, and in the little leisure of the morning, I see him still hard at work for the good of his pupils. Perhaps he is surrounded by a circle of the larger scholars, whom he has invited to spend the evening with him, to receive a more thorough explanation of some branch or item of study than there was time for in school. But stop — Mr. Henry did not keep the district school as it *was* — why, then, am I describing him?

Chapter XXI

The Examination at the Closing of the School

THE district school as it was, generally closed, in the winter, with what was called an " Examination." This was usually attended by the minister of the town, the committee who engaged the teacher, and such of the parents as chose to come in. Very few, however, were sufficiently interested in the improvement of their children, to spend three uncomfortable hours in the hot and crowded school-room, listening to the same dull round of words, year after year. If the school had been under the care of a good instructor, all was well of course; if a poor one, it was too late to help it. Or, perhaps, they thought they could not afford the time on a fair afternoon; and, if the weather was stormy, it was rather more agreeable to stay at home; besides, " Nobody else will be there, and why should I go ? " Whether such were the reflections of parents or not, scarcely more than half of them, at most, ever

attended the examination. I do not recollect
that the summer school was examined at all.
I know not the reason of this omission, unless
it was that such had been the custom from time
immemorial.

We shall suppose it to be the last day of the
winter school. The scholars have on their
better clothes, if their parents are somewhat
particular, or if the every-day dress " looks quite
too bad." The young ladies, especially, wear
the next best gown, and a more cleanly and
tastefully worked neckerchief. Their hair dis-
plays more abundant curls and a more elaborate
adjustment.

It is noon. The school-room is undergoing
the operation of being swept as clean as a worn-
out broom in the hands of one girl, and hemlock twigs in the hands of others, will permit.
Whew — what a dust ! Alas for Mary's cape,
so snow-white and smooth in the morning !
Hannah's curls, which lay so close to each
other, and so pat and still on her temples, have
got loose by the exercise, and have stretched
themselves into the figure of half-straightened
cork-screws, nearly unfit for service. The spirit
of the house-wife dispossesses the bland and smil-
ing spirit of the school-girl. The masculine can-
didates for matrimony can now give a shrewd

guess who are endued with an innate propensity to
scold; who will be Xantippes to their husbands,
should they ever get their Cupid's nests made
up again so as to catch them. " Be still, Sam,
bringing in snow," screams Mary. " Get away
boys, off out doors, or I'll sweep you into the
fire," snaps out Hannah, as she brushes the
urchins' legs with her hemlock. " There, take
that," screeches Margaret, as she gives a pro-
voking lubber a knock with a broom handle;
" there, take that, and keep your wet, dirty feet
down off the seats."

The sweeping and scolding are at length done.
The girls are now brushing their clothes, by
flapping handkerchiefs over themselves and each
other. The dust is subsiding; one can almost
breathe again. The master has come, all so
prim, with his best coat and a clean cravat;
and, may be, a collar is stiff and high above it.
His hair is combed in its genteelest curvatures.
He has returned earlier than usual, and the boys
are cut short in their play, — the glorious fun
of the last noon time. But they must all come
in. But what shall the visitors sit on ? " Go
up to Capt. Clark's, and borrow some chairs,"
says the master. Half a dozen boys are off in
a moment, and next, more than half a dozen
chairs are sailing, swinging, and clattering

through the air, and set in a row round the spelling-floor.

The school are at length all seated at their books, in palpitating expectation. The master makes a speech on the importance of speaking up, "loud and distinct," and of refraining from whispering, and all other things well known to be forbidden. The writing-books and ciphering manuscripts are gathered and piled on the desk, or the bench near it. "Where is your manuscript, Margaret?" "I carried it home last night." "Carried it home!—what's that for?" "'Cause I was ashamed on't—I haven't got half so far in 'rethmetic as the rest of the girls who cipher, I've had to stay at home so much."

A heavy step is heard in the entry. All is hushed within. They do nothing but breathe. The door opens—it is nobody but one of the largest boys who went home at noon. There are sleigh-bells approaching,—hark, do they stop? yes, up in Capt. Clark's shed. Now there is another tread, then a distinct and confident rap. The master opens the door, and the minister salutes him, and, advancing, receives the simultaneous bows and courtesies of the awed ranks in front. He is seated in the most conspicuous and honorable place, perhaps in the magisterial desk. Then some of the neighbors scatter in, and receive the same homage, though it is proffered with a more careless action and aspect.

Now commences the examination. First, the younger classes read and spell. Observe that little fellow, as he steps from his seat to take his place on the floor. It is his day of public triumph, for he is at the head; he has been there the most times, and a ninepence swings by a flaxen string from his neck. His skin wants letting out, it will hardly hold the important young gentleman. His mother told him this morning, when he left home, "to speak up like a minister," and his shrill oratory is almost at the very pinnacle of utterance.

The third class have read. They are now spelling. They are famous orthographers; the mightiest words of the spelling columns do not intimidate them. Then come the numbers, the abbreviations, and the punctuation. Some of the little throats are almost choked by the hurried ejection of big words and stringy sentences.

The master has gone through with the several accomplishments of the class. They are about to take their seats. " Please to let them stand a few moments longer, I should like to put out a few words to them, myself," says the minister. Now look out. They expect words as long as their finger, from the widest columns of the spelling-book, or perhaps such as are found only in the dictionary. "Spell *wrist*," says he to the little sweller at the head. "O, what an easy word!" r-i-s-t, wrist. It is not right. The next, the next — they all try, or rather do not attempt the word; for if r-i-s-t does not spell *wrist*, they cannot conceive what does. "Spell *gown*, Anna." G-o-u-n-d. "O no, it is *gown*, not *gound*. The next try." None of them can spell this. He then puts out *penknife*, which is spelt without the k, and then *andiron*, which his honor at the head rattles off in this way, " h-a-n-d hand, i-u-r-n hand iurn."

The poor little things are confused as well as discomfited. They hardly know what it means. The teacher is disconcerted and mortified. It dawns on him, that, while he has been following the order of the book, and priding himself that so young scholars can spell such monstrous great words, — words which perhaps they will never use, they cannot spell the names of the most familiar objects. The minister has taught him a lesson.

The writing-books are now examined. The mighty pile is lifted from the desk, and scattered along through the hands of the visitors. Some are commended for the neatness with which they have kept their manuscripts; some, for improvement in writing; of some, probably of the majority, is said nothing at all.

"Whew!" softly breathed the minister, as he opened a writing-book, some of whose pages were a complete ink-souse. He looked on the outside, and Simon Patch was the name that lay sprawling in the dirt which adhered to the newspaper cover. Simon spied his book in the reverend gentleman's hands, and noticed his queer stare at it. The minister looked up; Simon shrunk and looked down, for he felt that his eye was about to seek him. He gazed intensely in the book before him without seeing a word, at the same time earnestly sucking the pointed lapel of his Sunday coat. But Simon escaped without any audible rebuke.

Now comes the arithmetical examination; that is, the proficients in this branch are required to say the rules. Alas me! I had no reputation at all in this science. I could not repeat more than half the rules I had been over, nor more than the half of that half in the words of the book, as others could. What shame and confusion of face were mine on the last day, when we came to be questioned in Arithmetic! But when Mr. Ellis had his examination, I looked up a little, and felt that I was not so utterly incompetent as my previous teachers, together with myself, had supposed.

Then came the display in Grammar, our knowledge of which is especially manifested in parsing. A piece is selected which we have parsed in the course of the school, and on which we are again drilled so as to become as familiar with the parts of speech, and the governments and agreements of which, as we are with the buttons and button-holes of our jackets. We appear, of course, amazingly expert.

We exhibited our talent at Reading, likewise, in passages selected for the occasion, and conned over, and read over, until the dullest might call all the words right, and the most careless mind all the " stops and marks."

But this examination was a stupid piece of business to me. The expectation and preparation were somewhat exhilarating, as I trust has been perceived; but, as soon as the anticipated scene had commenced, it grew dull, and still more dull.

But let us finish this examination, now we are about it. Suppose it finished then. The minister remarks to the teacher, "Your school appears very well, in general, sir "; then he makes a speech, then a prayer, and his business is done. So is that of schoolmaster and school.

L

" You are dismissed," is uttered for the last
time this season. It is almost dark, and but
little time left for a last trip-up, snow-ball, or
slide down hill. The little boys and girls, with
their books and dinner baskets, ride home with
their parents, if they happen to be there. The
larger ones have some last words and laughs,
together, and then they leave the Old School-
house till December comes round again.

Chapter XXII

The Old School-house again — its Appearance the Last Winter — why so long occupied — a New One at last

MY first chapter was about the Old School-house: so shall be my last. The declining condition in which we first found it, has waxed into exceeding infirmity by the changes of thirteen years. After the summer school succeeding my thirteenth winter of district education, it was sold and carried piece-meal away, ceasing forever from the form and name of school-house.

I would have my readers see how the long-used and hard-used fabric appeared and how near to dissolution it came before the district could agree to accommodate their children with a new one.

We will now suppose it is my last winter at our school. Here we are inside, let us look around a little.

The long writing-benches arrest our attention as forcibly as anything in sight. They

were originally of substantial plank, an inch
and a half thick. And it is well that they were
thus massive. No board of ordinary measure
would have stood the hackings and hewings,
the scrapings and borings, which have been in-
flicted on those sturdy plank. In the first place,
the edge next the scholar is notched from end
to end, presenting an appearance something
like a broken-toothed mill-saw. Upon the
upper surface, there has been carved, or pictured with ink, the likeness of all things in the
heavens and on earth ever beheld by a country
school-boy; and sundry guesses at things he
never did see. Fifty years has this poor timber
been subjected to the knives of idlers, and
fully the fourth of fifty I have hacked on it
myself; and by this last winter their width has
become diminished nearly one-half. There are,
moreover, innumerable writings on the benches
and ceilings. On the boys' side were scribbled
the names of the Hannahs, the Marys, and the
Harriets, toward whom young hearts were beginning to soften in the first gentle meltings
of love. One would suppose that a certain
Harriet A., was the most distinguished belle the
district has ever produced, from the frequency
of her name on bench and wall.

The cracked and patched and puttied windows

are now still more diversified by here and there
a square of board instead of glass.

The master's desk is in pretty good order.
The first one was knocked over in a noon-time
scuffle, and so completely shattered as to render
a new one necessary. This has stood about
ten years.

As to the floor, had it been some winters we
could not have seen it without considerable
scraping away of dust and various kinds of litter;
for a broom was not always provided, and boys
would not wallow in the snow after hemlock,
and sweeping could not so well be done with a
stick. This winter, however, Mr. Ellis takes
care that the floor shall be visible the greater
part of the time. It is rough with sundry patches
of board nailed over chinks and knot-holes made
by the wear and tear of years.

Now we will look at the fire-place. One
end of the hearth has sunk an inch and a half
below the floor. There are crevices between
some of the tiles, into which coals of fire sometimes drop and make the boys spring for snow.
The andirons have each lost a fore-foot, and the
office of the important member is supplied by
bricks which had been dislodged from the chimney-top. The fire-shovel has acquired by accident or age a venerable stoop. The tongs can

no longer be called a pair, for the lack of one of the fellow-limbs. The bar of iron running from jamb to jamb in front, — how it is bent and sinking in the middle, by the pressure of the sagging fabric above! Indeed the whole chimney is quite ruinous. The bricks are loose here and there in the vicinity of the fire-place; and the chimney-top has lost so much of its cement that every high wind dashes off a brick, rolling and sliding on the roof, and then tumbling to the ground, to the danger of cracking whatever heedless skull may happen in the way.

The window-shutters, after having shattered the glass by the slams of many years, have broken their own backs at length. Some have fallen to the ground, and are going the way of all things perishable. Others hang by a single hinge, which is likely to give way at the next high gale, and consign the dangling shutter to the company of its fellows below.

The clapboards are here and there loose, and dropping one by one from their fastenings. One of these thin and narrow appendages, sticking by a nail at one end, and loose and slivered at the other, sends forth the most ear-rending music to the skillful touches of the North-west. Indeed, so many are the avenues by which the wind passes in and out, and so various are the notes, according as the rushing air vibrates a splinter, makes the window clatter, whistles through a knot-hole, and rumbles like a big bass down the chimney, that the edifice may be imagined uproarious winter's Panharmonicon, played upon in turn by all the winds.

Such is the condition of the Old School-house, supposing it to be just before we leave it forever, at the close of my thirteenth and last winter at our district school. It has been resorted to summer after summer, and winter after winter, although the observation of parents and the sensations of children have long given evidence that it ought to be abandoned.

At every meeting on school affairs that has been held for several years, the question of a new school-house has been discussed. All agree on the urgent need of one, and all are willing to contribute their portion of the wherewith; but when they attempt to decide on its location, then their harmonious action is at an end. All know that this high bleak hill, the coldest spot within a mile, is not the place; it would be stupid folly to put it here. At the foot of the hill, on either side, is as snug and pleasant a spot as need be. But the East-enders will not permit its location on the opposite side, and the

West-enders are as obstinate on their part. Each division declares that it will secede and form a separate district should it be carried further off, although in this case they must put up with much cheaper teachers, or much less schooling, or submit to twice the taxes.

Thus they have tossed the ball of discussion, and sometimes hurled that of contention, back and forth, year after year, to just about as much profit as their children have flung snow-balls in play, or chips and cakes of ice when provoked. At length, Time, the final decider of all things material, wearied with their jars, is likely to end them by tumbling the old ruin about their ears.

Months have passed; it is near winter again. There is great rejoicing among the children, satisfaction among the parents, harmony between the two Ends. A new school-house has been erected at last — indeed it has. A door of reconciliation and mutual adjustment was opened in the following manner.

That powerful-to-do, but tardy personage, the Public, began to be weary of ascending and descending Capt. Clark's hill. He began to calculate the value of time and horse-flesh. One day it occurred to him that it would be as

" cheap, and indeed much cheaper," to go round
this hill at the bottom, than to go round it over
the top; for it is just as far from side to side of
a ball in one direction as in another, and this was
a case somewhat similar. He perceived that
there would be no more lost in the long run by
the expense of carrying the road an eighth of a
mile to the south, and all on level ground, than
there would be by still wasting the breath of
horse and the patience of man in panting up and
tottering down this monstrous hill. It seemed
as if he had been blind for years, not to have
conceived of the improvement before. No time
was to be lost now. He lifted up his many-
tongued voice, and put forth his many-handed
strength; and, in the process of a few months,
a road was constructed, curving round the south
side of the aforesaid hill, which, after all, proved
to be but a few rods longer from point to point
than the other.

The district were no longer at variance about
the long-needed edifice. The aforementioned
improvement had scarcely been decided on, before every one perceived how the matter might
be settled. A school-meeting was soon called,
and it was unanimously agreed to erect a new
school-house on the new road, almost exactly
opposite the old spot, and as equidistant from

the two Ends, it was believed, as the equator is
from the poles.

Here Mr. Henry *taught* the District School
somewhat as it should be; and it has never since
been *kept* as it was.

A SUPPLICATION TO THE PEOPLE OF THE UNITED STATES

A Supplication

ABOUT *sixty thousand Slaves*, owned by the *People* of the *United States*, make the following *supplication* to their masters, not for *emancipation*, but for the *amelioration* of the condition of certain individuals of their race.

MOST SOVEREIGN, RIGHTFUL, AND EXCELLENT MASTERS, — We are the *English Language*, — your lawful and perpetual bond-servants, whose names and origin, characters and duties, are so faithfully exhibited, in Noah Webster's great Dictionary. By far the largest part of us have received nothing but the kindest usage from our owners, from time immemorial. Some thousands of us, indeed, were it possible, might die of having nothing to do but sleep, shut up in the dormitory of the Dictionary, or in the composition of some most learned, or most silly book, which the mass of the people never open. But of this we do not complain. Nor do we account it much of an evil, that certain Yankees make us weary, with the monstrously long drawl with which they articulate us into use. Nor do we cry out against the painful clipping, cutting-up, and shattering-to-pieces, given us by the African race; — for we serve them as faithfully as we do their white fellow-mortals.

But now we humbly pray that you will hear what we do complain of. We complain, that certain of our brethren are exceedingly abused, and made wretched, by some thousands, and perhaps millions, of our owners. Their piteous groans have shocked our ears, — their unretrieved sufferings have pained our sympathizing hearts, for many years. We can endure no longer; — we *must* speak. Your ancient servants come, then, supplicating you to take measures for the relief of the sufferings of the individuals of our number, whose names and particular subjects of complaint shall now be enumerated, proceeding in alphabetical order.

Arithmetic, — that accurate calculator, indispensable to this mighty and money-making nation, grievously complains that he is obliged to work for thousands without the use of A-head, and deprived of one of his two *i*'s. Here is a picture of his mutilated form, — *Rethmetic!*

Attacked, — an important character, that figures so gloriously in military dispatches, and is so necessary in medical reports, — is forced, by many, to the use of *t*, more than his constitution

will admit. He cannot perform his necessary
business, you know, without the use of *t*, twice
during every job, — but to have it forced into
him three times, causes a change in his constitution and appearance, which he cannot comforta-
bly bear. See how *Attacked* is altered by more
t than he wants, — *Attack Ted*.

There is another poor fellow, who has a similar affliction, — *Across*. See what a spectacle a
little *t* makes of him, — *Acrosst*.

That most excellent friend and profitable
servant of the Workingmen's party, *Earn*,
complains that those whom he serves the best,
deprive him of what little *e's* his laborious condition demands. See what *Earn* is brought to
by such hard treatment, — *Airn*.

That necessary attendant on every messenger,
— *Errand*, is in the same state of suffering, from
the same cause. *Errand* is made *Arrant*.

After — is willing to linger behind everybody
else in his business; but it is a miserable fate
to be deprived of so large a portion of his small
energy in this way, — *Arter*.

" Go *arter* the cows, Tom," says Ma'am Milk-
moolly. " I move that we adjourn to *arternoon*,"
says Squire Goodman, in the Legislature.

Hear, also, how that entirely different character, and bold goer-ahead, growls as he passes on,

— *Before.* " I will go forward and do my duty as long as any part of me is left sound; but my well-being is dreadfully affected by a great many people whom I serve, — as you cannot but perceive," — *Afore.*

Bellows, — that excellent household servant, — says he has often had his nose stopped up by ashes, and has wheezed with the asthma for months, but all these afflictions are nothing to usage like this, — *Belluses.*

Bachelor — is exceedingly sensitive about what is said of him in the presence of the ladies. He is shockingly mortified at being called *Batchelder.* To be sure, he is a batch-*elder* than he ought to be, regarding the comfort of maidens and the good of his country; but he is an odd fellow, and wants his own way. He is almost tempted to destroy himself by taking that deadly poison to his nature, — *a wife,* — in order to be relieved from his mortification.

Boil — is at the hot duty of keeping the pot going, and sometimes it is hard work; however, he complains not of this; but poor *Boil* has had the jaundice, and all other liver complaints, for years, and is *blubbering* like a baby — all in consequence of this, viz., about nine-tenths of the cooks in America, and two-thirds of the eaters, call him *Bile.*

Cellar — is the lowest character in the house, and takes more wine and cider than any other, and is the *biggest sauce-box* in the world. Yet, with all the propriety of the parlor, and a sobriety, as if not a drop of intoxicating liquor was in him, he now implores you to remember that he is a *Cellar*, and not a *Suller*.

Chimney. — Here is a character who ten thousand times would have taken fire at an affront, were it not for the danger of burning up the houses and goods of his abusers, — faithful servant and tender-hearted creature that he is! He is content to do the hottest, hardest, and dirtiest work in the world. You may put as much green wood upon his back as you please, and make him breathe nothing but smoke, and swallow nothing but soot, and stand over steam, till pots and kettles boil no more; all these are ease, pleasantness, and peace, to abuse like this, — *Chimbly.*

Dictionary — rages with all the rough epithets in gentlemanly or vulgar use; and then he melts into the most tender and heart-moving words of entreaty, and, in fact, tries all the various powers of the English language. Still further, mighty lexicographic champions, such as Dr. Webster, Sheridan, Walker, Perry, Jones, Fulton and Knight, and Jameson, besides numerous

M

other inferior defenders, — even hosts of spelling-book makers, have all exerted their utmost
in vain, to save him from the ignominy of being
— *Dicksonary*.

End — is uttering the most dolorous groans.
There are certain individuals who are always
killing him without putting him to an *end*. See
what a torture he is put to — *eend, eend*.

Further, — that friend of the progress and
improvements of this ahead-going age, stops by
the way to ask relief. He is ready to further
all the innumerable plans for the benefit of man,
except when he is *brought back* in this way —
Furder.

General, — that renowned and glorifying character, whose fame has resounded through the
world, is dishonored and made gloryless by many
a brave man as well as chicken-heart. He has
now intrenched himself in this position, viz.,
that he will no longer magnify many little
militia-folks into mightiness, unless they forbear
to call him *Gineral*. It is not only a degradation, but it is an offence to his associations.
Gin — *Gin*-er-al; *Wine*-er-al, and much more,
Water-al, would be more glory-giving in these
un-treating, or rather, re-treating times of
temperance.

Gave, — that generous benefactor, that magnanimous philanthropist, is almost provoked. He declares that he has a good mind, for once, to demand back his donations from the temper-trying miscallers. I gave a thousand dollars, this very day, towards the completion of Bunker-Hill Monument. But don't say of me, he *gin*. I never *gin* a cent in my life.

Get, — that enterprising and active character, who is a stanch friend of all the temperate and industrious, stops to complain, that some of those he serves the best call him — *Git*. And he is very reluctant to get along about his business, till some measures are taken to prevent the abuse. *Get* is now waiting, ye workers of all professions; what say? Will you still, with a merciless *i*, make him *Git*?

Gum — is always on the *jaw*, that he is so often called *Goomb*, in spite of his teeth.

Gown, — that very ladylike personage, is sighing away at the deplorable *de*-formity that *de*-spoils her beauty in the extreme, as is *de*-veloped in the following *de-tail*, *Gown-d*. Oh! ye lords of language! if ye have any gallantry, come to the deliverance of the amiable *gown*, that she may shake off this D-pendant.

Handkerchief, — your personal attendant, is also distressed in the *extreme*. She is kept by many from her *chief* end in the following cruel manner — *Handker*-CHER.

January, — that old Roman, is storming away in the most bitter wrath; shaking about his snowy locks, and tearing away at his icy beard, like a madman. " Blast 'em," roars his Majesty of midwinter, " don't they know any better than to call me *Jinuary?* They say, ' It is a terrible cold J*i*nuary,' — then, ' It is the J*i*nuary thaw.' Oh! ye powers of the air! help me to freeze and to melt them by turns, every day, for a month, until they shall feel the difference between the vowel *a*, and the vowel *i*. My name is *January*."

Kettle, — that faithful kitchen-servant, is boiling with rage. He is willing to be hung in trammels, and be obliged to get his living by hook and by crook, and be hauled over the coals every day, and take even pot-luck for his fare, — and, indeed, to be called black by the pot; — all this he does not care a snap for; but to be called *Kittle* — KITTLE! " Were it not for the stiffness of my limbs, I would soon take leg-*bail*," says the fiery hot *Kettle*.

Little — allows that he is a very inferior character, but avers that he is not *least* in the great nation of words. He cannot be *more*, and he will not be *less*. Prompted by a considerate self-respect, he informs us that he is degraded to an unwarrantable diminutiveness by being called — *Leetle*. " A *leetle* too much," says one. " A *leetle* too far," says another. " A mighty *leetle* thing," cried a third. Please to call respectable adjectives by their right names, is the polite request of your humble servant, *Little*.

Lie, — that verb of so quiet a disposition by nature, is roused to complain that his repose is exceedingly disturbed in the following manner. Almost the whole American nation, learned as well as unlearned, have the inveterate habit of saying — *Lay*, when they mean, and might say — *Lie*. " *Lay* down, and *lay* abed, and let it *lay*," is truly a national sin against the laws of grammar.

Mrs., — that respectable abbreviation, is exceedingly grieved at the indignity she suffers. The good ladies, whom she represents, are let down from the matronly dignity, to which she would hold them, even to the un-married degradation of *Miss*; — and this in the United States, where matrimony is so universally honored and sought after. She desires it to be universally published, that *Miss* belongs only to ladies who have never been blessed with husbands.

Oil, — you all know, has a disposition, smooth to a proverb; — but he is, to say the least, in great danger of losing his fine, easy temper, by being treated in the altogether improper manner that you here behold — *Ile !*

Potatoes, — (those most indispensable servants to all dinner-eating Americans, and the benevolent furnishers of "*daily bread*," and, indeed, the whole living to Pat-land's poor,) — *Potatoes*, are weeping with all their *eyes*, at the agony to which they are put by thousands. They are most unfeelingly mangled, top and toe, in this manner, — *Taters*. Notwithstanding their *extremities*, in the most *mealy*-mouthed manner they exclaim, — "Po! Po! gentlemen and ladies! pray spare us a head, and you may bruise our *toes* in welcome. Still, you must confess that *Potaters* is not so sound and *whole*-some as *Potatoes*."

Point — allows that in some respects he is of very minute importance; but asserts that in others he is of the greatest consequence, as in an argument, for instance. *Point* is determined to prick forward in the cause, till he shall be no longer blunted and turned away from his aim, and robbed of his very nature, in the *measure* you here perceive — *Pint*.

Philadelphia — takes off his broad-brim, and,

in the softest tones of brotherly love, implores
the people of the United States to cease calling
him by that harsh, horrid, and un-brotherly
name, — *Fellydelphy*. It deprives him of his
significance, and ancient and honorable lineage,
as every Greek scholar well knows.

Poetry. — What a halo of glory around this
daughter of Genius, and descendant of Heaven!
Behold how she is rent asunder by many a pitiful proser, and made to come *short* of due honor.
Potry — Apollo and the Muses know nothing
about *Potry!*

Quench, — that renowned extinguisher, whom
all the world can't hold a candle to, is himself
very much *put out,* now and then, from this cause,
— some people permit that crooked and hissing
serpent *S*, to get before him, and coil round
him, while he is in the hurry of duty, as you
here see — *Squench;* and sometimes they give
him a horrid black *i*, thus — *Squinch*.

Rather — is universally known to be very
nice in his preferences, and to be almost con-
tinually occupied in expressing them. Be it as
universally known, then, that he is disgusted
beyond all bearing at being called — *Ruther*.

Sauce — has a good many elements in him,
and, above all, a proper share of self-respect.
He thinks he has too much spice and spirit to

be considered such a flat as this indicates —
Sass.

Scarce — is not a very frequent complainant
of anything, — but he now complains of certain
Nippies, both male and female, and hosts of
honest imitators, call him *Scurce*, thinking it the
very tip of gentility.

Such — does not complain of mistaken polite-
ness, but of low and vulgar treatment like this
— *Sich*.

Since — embraces all antiquity, goes back beyond Adam, yea, as far back into the unbegin-
ningness as you could think in a million of
years, and unimaginably further. And, oh!
his hoary head is bowed down with sorrow
at being called by two-thirds of the American
people, *Sence*.

Spectacles, — those twin literati, who are ever
poring over the pages of learning, raise eyes of
supplication. They say that they cannot *look*
with due respect upon certain elderly people,
who *pronounce* them more unlettered than they
really are, as you may perceive without looking
with their interested eyes — *Spetacles*. Venerable
friends, pray *c* us, *c* us.

Sit — has been provoked to stand up in his
own behalf, although he is of sedentary habits,
and is sometimes inclined to be idle. He de-

clares he has too much pride and spirit to let
that more active personage — *Set* — do all his
work for him. " *Set* still," says the pedagogue
to his pupils — and parents to their children.
" *Set* down, sir," — say a thousand gentlemen,
and some famously learned ones, to their visitors. " The coat *sets* well," affirms the tailor.
Now all this does not *sit* well on your complainant, and he *sets* up his Ebenezer, that he
should like a little more to do, — especially in
the employ of college-learned men, and also of
the teachers of American youth.

Sat — makes grievous complaint that he is
called *Sot*. He begs all the world to know that
he hath not redness of eyes, nor rumminess nor
brandiness of breath, nor flamingness of nose,
that he should be degraded by the drunkard's
lowest and last name — *Sot*.

Shut. — This is a person of some importance.
He is, indeed, the most decisive and unyielding
exclusive in the world. He keeps the outs, out,
and the ins, in, both in fashionable and political
life. Now this stiff old aristocrat is made to
appear exceedingly flat, silly, and undignified, by
being called, by sundry persons, — *Shet*. " *Shet*
the door," says old Grandsire Grumble, of a
cold, windy day. " *Shet* your books," says the
schoolmaster, when he is about to hear the

urchins spell. "*Shet* up, you saucy blockhead," cries he, to young Insolence. This is too bad! It is abominable! a schoolmaster, the appointed keeper of orthographical and orthoëpical honor, — letting fall the well-bred and lofty-minded — *Shut* — from his guardian lips, in the shape of *Shet*. Oh! the plebeian! Faithless and unfit pedagogue!! He ought to be banished to Shet-land, where by day he should battle with Boreas; and where by night his bed should be the summit of a snow-drift, — his sheets nothing but Arctic mists, — and his pillow the fragment of an iceberg!! Away with the traitor to *Shet*-land! O, most merciful American masters and mistresses! *Shut* has no relief or safety from the miserableness of Shet, but in U.

Told — feels the dignity of his vocation, and asks not to be kept out of use by such bad grammar as this — *Telled*.

Yes, — that good-natured personage, affirms that were he not of so complying a disposition, he would henceforth be *no* to everybody who should call him — *Yis*.

Finally, — hearken! There is a voice from the past. It is the complaint of departing *Yesterday*. He cries aloud — Give ear, O, To-day, and hear, hear, O, To-morrow! Never, never more, call me *Yisterday*!

We have thus presented you, Sovereign Owners, with the complaints and groans of a considerable number of our race.   There are,
doubtless, many others, who are also in a state
of suffering, but who have uncommon fortitude,
or too much modesty, to come forward publicly, and make known their trials to our whole
assembled community.   Should the abuse of any
such happen to be known to you at any time, we
pray that the same consideration may be given
to them as to the rest.

Now, Sovereign Masters and Mistresses, and
Rightful Owners, shall these visions of hope be
realized ?   Shall the condition of our suffering
brethren be ameliorated ?   Shall the era of good
grammar, correct spelling, and proper pronunciation, be hastened forward by some benevolent
exertions ?   Shall the present abuses be trans-
mitted to the future or not ?   Shall the Golden
Age of Speech speedily come, and last evermore ?

That such improvement in their condition
may be vouchsafed, is the humble prayer of
your supplicants ; — all whose names, being too
numerous to be here subscribed, may be found
recorded in Webster's great Dictionary.

PAGES FROM OLD SPELLERS

FRONTISPIECE OF "THE ONLY SURE GUIDE."
(See page 11.)

THE ALPHABET.

Roman.		Italic.		Names.	Numbers.
A	a	*A*	*a*	*a*	1
B	b	*B*	*b*	*bee*	2
C	c	*C*	*c*	*see*	3
D	d	*D*	*d*	*dee*	4
E	e	*E*	*e*	*e*	5
F	f	*F*	*f*	*eff*	6
G	g	*G*	*g*	*jee*	7
H	h	*H*	*h*	*aitch*	8
I	i	*I*	*i*	*i*	9
J	j	*J*	*j*	*jay*	10
K	k	*K*	*k*	*kay*	11
L	l	*L*	*l*	*el*	12
M	m	*M*	*m*	*em*	13
N	n	*N*	*n*	*en*	14
O	o	*O*	*o*	*o*	15
P	p	*P*	*p*	*pee*	16
Q	q	*Q*	*q*	*cue*	17
R	r	*R*	*r*	*ar*	18
S	s	*S*	*s*	*ess*	19
T	t	*T*	*t*	*tee*	20
U	u	*U*	*u*	*u*	21
V	v	*V*	*v*	*vee*	22
W	w	*W*	*w*	*double u*	23
X	x	*X*	*x*	*eks*	24
Y	y	*Y*	*y*	*wy*	25
Z	z	*Z*	*z*	*zee or zed*	26

Lesson 1

bā	bē	bī	bō	bū	bȳ
ćā	ćē	ćī	ćō	ćū	ćȳ
dā	dē	dī	dō	dū	dȳ
fā	fē	fī	fō	fū	fȳ
gā	gē	gī	gō	gū	gȳ
hā	hē	hī	hō	hū	hȳ

Lesson 2.

jā	jē	jī	jō	jū	jȳ
kā	kē	kī	kɔ	kū	kȳ
lā	lē	lī	lō	lū	lȳ
mā	mē	mī	mó	mū	mȳ
nā	nē	nī	nō	nū	nȳ
pā	pē	pi	pō	pū	pȳ

Lesson 3.

rā	rē	rī	rō	rū	rȳ
sā	sē	sī	sō	sū	sȳ
tā	tē	tī	tō	tū	tȳ
vā	vē	vī	vō	vū	vȳ
wā	wē	wi	wó	wū	wȳ
zā	zē	zī	zō	zū	zȳ

Lesson 4.

ăb	ĕb	ĭb	ŏb	ŭb	hē
ăć	ĕć	ĭć	ŏć	ŭć	ĭſ
ăd	ĕd	ĭd	ŏd	ŭd	ŭp
ăſ	ĕf	ĭf	ŏſ	ŭf	wē
ăg	ĕg	ĭg	ŏg	ŭg	gō
ăl	ĕl	ĭl	ŏl	ŭl	ĭn

Lesson 5

ăm	ĕm	ĭm	ŏm	ŭm	sō
ăn	ĕn	ĭn	ŏn	ŭn	hē
ăp	ĕp	ĭp	ŏp	ŭp	ĭſ

broâd	fáŭlt	háŭght	wârd	wârt
fraŭd	vâŭlt	tâŭght	swârd	thwârt
ēach	ēve	blēach	chēēk	fēē
rēach	hēave	prēach	shriĕk	trēē
ēaše	bēad	brēam	chēēše	fiĕf
plēaše	plēad	strēam	lēēš	chiĕf
ēast	bēak	brēaтне	člēave	fiērče
lēast	pēak	shēaтне	thiĕve	piērče
ēĕl	bēēveš	briĕf	črēase	flēēče
fĕĕl	grēaveš	shēaf	grēase	gēēse
grēaše*	kēēp	lēēr	plēa	rēar
snēēze	slēēp	mēre	pēa	spēar
hēat	knēē	kiĕǧē	pēat	rēĕl
nĕat	tēa	siĕǧē	sēat	tēal
hēath	lēan	nĕap	sēēk	sčhēme
shēath	yēan	pēēp	slēĕk	thēme
kēēl	lēēch	quēēr	shē	spēak
knēēl	pēach	smēar	thrēē	squēak
sčrēēn	tēēth	snēĕr	tēaše	chirp
splēēn	wrēath	sphēre	тнēše	stirp
strēam	shiĕld	squēal	trēat	ĕarth
strēam	wiĕld	whēēl	whēat	dēarth
sčrēēch	slēēt	squēēze	twēak	ĕdǧe
spēēch	strēēt	whēēze	strēak	drēdǧe
sēēтн	snēak	stēēd	wĕnčh	ĕrr
wrēaтн	spēak	wēēd	wrĕnčh	fir
irk	člĕanšc	ǧĕrm	ǧirt	hĕrn
jĕrk	lĕnš	firm	wĕrt	yēarn
brĕast	dĕaf	flĕdǧe	hĕad	hĕlp
vĕst	fĕoff	plĕdǧe	thrĕad	whĕlp
brĕath	gĕt	shĕrd	hĕalth	pĕrk

* A verb.

DUTIES OF CHILDREN.

Love your brothers and sisters. Do not tease nor vex them, nor call them names; and never let your little hands be raised to strike them. If they have any thing which you would like to have, do not be angry with them, nor try to get it from them. If you have any thing they like, share it with them.

Your parents grieve when they see you quarrel; they love you all, and wish you to love one another, and to live in peace and harmony.

Do not meddle with what does not belong to you; nor ever take other people's things without leave.

Never tell an untruth. When you are relating any thing you have seen, or heard, endeavour to tell it exactly as it was. Do not alter or invent any part, or make it, as you may think, a prettier story. If you have forgotten any part, say that you have forgotten it.

Persons who love the truth, never tell a lie even in jest.

WORDS OF THREE SYLLABLES.

ā	ā′rī̯ē̠s̈	drā′pĕr-y̆
a′ğĕn-c̆y̆	ā′thē-ĭsm	l̆igh′tĭ-ĕth
a′lĭ-ăs	bā′yŏn-ĕt	fā′vŏur-ĭte
al′ĭĕn-āte	brā′vĕr-y̆	fĕign′ĕd-ly̆
a′ō-rĭst	c̆ā′vē-ăt	flā′grăn-cy̆
a′prĭ-c̆ŏt	chānge′ā-ble	gāi′ē-ty̆
a′quē-ŏus	dāi′ry̆-māid	grāte′fŭl-ly̆
a′rē-ā	dăn′ğĕr-ŏus	gŭā′lĭ-c̆ŭm
hĕi′nŏus-nĕss	pā′pă-cy̆	rā′dĭ-ŭs
knā′vĕr-y̆	pā′trĭ-àrch	rā′pĭ-ĕr
lā′ĭ-ty̆	pā′trĭ-ŏt	rā′tă-ble
lā′zĭ-nĕss	pā′trŏn-ĕss	rā′tĭ-ō
māle′c̆ŏn-tĕnt	phā′ē-tŏn	sāle′ā-ble
mā′nĭ-ăc̆	plā′c̆ă-ble	sā′pĭ-ĕnce
nāl′ā-dē̈s̈	plā′ğiă-rĭsm	sā′tĭ-āte
pā′găn-ĭsm	rā′dĭ-ănce	sā′vŏr-y̆

crȳs-tăl-lĭ-zā'tĭŏn	e-măn-cĭ-pā'tĭŏn
dē-nŭn-cĭ-ā'tĭŏn	ĕn-thū-sĭ-ăs'tĭk
dē-sĭd-ē-rā'tŭm	ĕp-ĭ-cū-rē'an
dĭ-ăph-ō-rĕt'ĭk	ĕx-ăg-gē-rā'tĭŏn
ĕc-clē-sĭ-ăs'tĭk	ĕx-pŏst-ū-lā'tĭŏn
ĕd-ĭ-fĭ-kā'tĭŏn	gē-ŏm-ē-trĭ-cĭ'an
ē-jăc-ū-lā'tĭŏn	gĕs-tĭc-ū-lā'tĭŏn
ē-lū-cĭ-dā'tĭŏn	hī-ē-rō-glȳph'ĭk
ĭ-măg-ĭn-ā'tĭŏn	mē-tĕmp-sȳ-chō'sĭs
ĭn-âū-gŭ-rā'tĭŏn	nē-gō-tĭ-ā'tĭŏn
ĭn-dĭs-pō-sĭ-tĭ'ŏn	pă-pĭl-ĭŏ-nā'ceoŭs
ĭn-făt-'ū-ā'tĭŏn	phàr-mă-cō-poē'ĭa
ĭn-tĕr-rō-gā'tĭŏn	prē-cĭp-ĭ-tā'tĭŏn
ĭn-vĕs-tĭ-gā'tĭŏn	prō-nŭn-cĭ-ā'tĭŏn
jŭs-tĭ-fĭ-kā'tĭŏn	prŏs-ō-pō-poē'ĭa
măth-ē-mă-tĭ-cĭ'an	quăl-ĭ-fĭ-kā'tĭŏn
rĕc-'ŏm-mĕn-dā'tĭŏn	sŭb-tĭl-ĭ-zā'tĭŏn
rē-gĕn-ĕr-ā'tĭŏn	sŭ-pĕr-ĭn-tĕnd'ĕnce
rē-ĭt-'ĕr-ā'tĭŏn	sŭp-pŏṣ-ĭ-tĭ-tĭ'oŭs
rē-sŭs-cĭ-tā'tĭŏn	tĕr-gĭ-vĕr-sā'tĭŏn
rē-vĕr-bĕr-ā'tĭŏn	trăns-fĭg-ū-rā'tĭŏn
sănc-tĭ-fĭ-kā'tĭŏn	vĕr-sĭ-fĭ-cā'tĭŏn
sō-lĭc-ĭ-tā'tĭŏn	vĭv-ĭ-fĭ-kā'tĭŏn
stĕr-ē-ō-grăph'ĭk	vō-cĭf er-ā'tĭŏn
cŏn-cĭl'ĭ-ā-tŏr-ȳ	ĭn-tĕr-rŏg"ā-tŏr-ȳ
ē-jăc'ū-lā-tŏr-ȳ	ĭr-rē-cŏv'ĕr-ă-ble
prō-pĭ-tĭ"ĭ-ā-tŏr ȳ	ĭr-rē-mē'dĭ-ă-ble
rē-vĕr'bĕr-ă-tŏr-ȳ	sŭ-pĕr-nŭ'mĕr-ăr-ȳ
chrŏn-ō-lŏg'ĭ-căl-lȳ	thē-ō-rĕt'ĭ-căl-lȳ
cĭr-cŭm-lŏc'ū-tō-rȳ	ăd-mĭ-ră-bĭl"ĭ-tȳ
ĕle-ē-mŏṣ'ȳ-năr-ȳ	ăn-tē-mē-rĭ'dĭ-ăn
ĭn-de-făt''ĭ-ga-ble	ăn-tĭ-mō-năr-chĭ-căl

The Lord is God, and the only God. It is he that hath made us, and does us good.

The life of the body and the life of the soul are from God. He made the eye, and can see us. He made the ear, and can hear us. The eye of God is upon the evil, and the good.

If you love God he will save you. Make the word of God the rule of all you do; mind well what HE says in his word, for that will show you the way to life. This life is for a short time; but the life to come has no end.

Look at them that do well, and do so too. Keep from them that do evil and tell lies. Fear the Lord all the day long.

Let us love the Lord our God with all our soul; for he is kind to us. If the Lord keep us, we need not fear any evil.

We must hate no one; but love and do good to all; and love them that do not love us. Be just and kind to all men. It is the bad boy, that will hurt, when he can, his play-mate; you must not do it, if you can help it; no, you must not so much as vex him.

As soon as the sun is up, you must be up, and not lie in bed.

The sun was made for man and it will be of no use to him, if he is not up.

You are to lie down, and take rest in the night; but rise and work in the day.

QUESTIONS FOR LITTLE BOYS.

How many fingers have you got, little boy?
Here are four fingers on this hand. And what is this?
Thumb. Four fingers and thumb, that makes five. And how many on the other hand?
There are five too.
What is this?
This is the right hand.
And this? This is the left hand.
And how many toes have you got? Let us count.
Five upon this foot, and five upon that foot.
Five and five make ten : ten fingers and ten toes.
How many legs have you?
Here is one, and here is another. Charles has two legs.
How many legs has a horse?
A horse has four legs.
And how many has a dog?
Four ; and a cow has four ; and a sheep has four ; and puss has four legs.
And how many legs have the chickens?
Go and look.
The chickens have only two legs.
And the linnets, and the robins, and all the birds have only two legs.
But I will tell you what birds have got ; they have got wings to fly with, and they fly very high in the air.

THE GOOD CHILD.

Oh, that it were my chief delight
   To do the things I ought!
Then let me try with all my might
   To mind what I am taught.

Wherever I am told to go,
   I 'll cheerfully obey ;
Nor will I mind it much, although
   I leave a pretty play.

When I am bid. I'll freely bring
   Whatever I have got ;
Nor will I touch a pretty thing
   If mother tells me not.

When she permits me, I may tell
   About my pretty toys ;
But if she's busy, or unwell,
   I must not make a noise.

And when I learn my hymns to say,
   And work and read and spell,
I will not think about my play,
   But try and do it well.

For GOD looks down from heaven on high,
   Our actions to behold,
And he is pleased, when children try
   To do as they are told.

THE GOOD SCHOLAR

Joseph West had been told,
That if, when he grew old,
He had not learned rightly to spell,
Though his writing were good,
'Twould not be understood:
And Joe said, " I will learn my task well."

And he made it a rule
To be silent at school;
And what do you think came to pass?
Why, he learned it so fast,
That, from being the last,
He soon was the first in the class.

SELECT SENTENCES.

Never ask other persons to do any thing for you, which you can as properly do for yourself.

As soon as you have learned to work well, try to work quick.

If we do not take pains, we must not expect to excel in any thing.

Attentive and industrious people can always find time to do what is proper for them to do.

Sec. 15.

Sweet, Sweet-er, Sweet-est.

A pear is sweet, a plumb is sweeter, honey is sweetest.

Ann is a **sweet** child — She does not cry or snarl. She minds her pa and ma, and loves the little babe. So she is a **sweet** child.

The robin sings **sweet-ly.** You have seen the rob-in sit-ting on a limb, and heard her sweet song.

The sap of the ma-ple has **sweet-ness.** It can be boil-ed till only the sweetness is left, and then it is sugar.

Sweet, sweeter, sweet-est, sweet-ly, sweet-ness.
Bold, bolder, bold-est, bold-ly, boldness.

cold	wild	high	calm	harsh
blind	light	bright	dark	sharp
mild	tight	kind	hard	smart

Sec. 18.

Now you know so many words, you can read a story about the boy who stole a pin. But first can you tell me what is a pin? Of what is it made? What kind of wire?— What is done to the ends? For what is it used? Now hear the story about

The boy who stole a pin.

A little while ago a good man went to the cold, dark jail, to talk with the wicked persons who were shut up there for crimes.— He found one man, who was soon to be hung. He was taken up for rob-bing, tried by the court, and con-dem-ned to be hung. The good man asked him how he came to such an end. Said the rob-ber, "The first thing that led me to it was, when I was a little boy and went to school, *I stole a pin.* I saw it on the coat-cuff of the boy who sat next to me, and I want-ed it. But I was afraid to take it because it was none of mine. I looked at it again, and wished it were mine. And when no one saw me, I put out my hand, and drew it from the cuff, and hid it behind me. But O! how I *felt!* It seemed to me all the boys in school look-ed right at me, and said, '*You stole a pin!*' What would I not have given, if it were

crime—some-thing wrong. What is a cuff?

stole a pin   to be hung.

back in the cuff. But I was ashamed to put it back, and let the boy know that I had stol-en it; so I kept it. I was not found out, and soon for-got how bad I felt. I then saw a knife, and wanted that. I felt more bold to take it, as I was not found out with the pin; so I took the knife. I did not feel quite so bad. Next, I stole a roll of cloth, and so went on from bad to worse, until I got me a pis-tol to get things by force. I went to a thick clump of bushes and hid till it was dark. Then as a man passed by, I jumped from my hiding place, held up my pistol, and told him to give me his mon-ey or he shot. He gave me his money; but I was soon found out and taken to jail. From there I was ta-ken to tri-al, and now am condemned to hang by a rope round the neck till I am dead. And it is all to be traced to this—

'I stole a pin!'

Here the good man left him to die.

Now tell me, my child, what is it to steal? What is it to rob?

If you have *done wrong*, do so *no more*.— Your sin will find you out.

Knife—what? How many parts—handle, spring, blade. Of what made and for what used?

6

LITTLE ANN.

Mother, how can the flowers grow ?
Said little Ann one day ;
The garden is all over snow ;
When will it go away ?

The sun, my love, will melt the snow,
And warm the frozen ground ;
But many a wintry wind will blow
Before the flowers are found

In a few months, my Ann will view
The garden now so white,
With yellow cowslip, violet blue,
And daffodil so bright.

The birds will then, from every tree,
  Pour forth a song of praise ;
Their little hearts will grateful be,
  And sweet will sound their lays.

For God, who dwells above the sky,
  Made them, as well as you ;
He gave them little wings to fly,
  And made their music too.

He gave my little girl her voice,
  To join in prayer and praise ;
Then may she ever more rejoice
  To learn her Maker's ways !

GEORGE WASHINGTON.

On a fine morning in the fall of 1737, Mr. Washington, having little George by the hand, came to the door and asked my cousin and myself to walk with him to the orchard, promising to show us a fine sight. On arriving at the orchard, we were presented with a fine sight indeed. The whole earth as far as we could see, was strewed with fruit : and yet the trees were bending under the weight of apples, which hung in clusters, like grapes, and vainly strove to hide their red cheeks behind the green leaves.

"Now, George," said his father, "look here, my son! don't you remember, when this good cousin of yours brought you that fine large apple, last spring, how hardly I could prevail on you to divide with your brothers and sisters; though I promised you that if you would but do it, God Almighty would give you plenty of apples, this fall?"

Poor George could not say a word; but, hanging down his head, looked quite confused, while with his little naked toes he scratched in the soft ground.—"Now look up, my son," continued his father, "and see how richly that blessed God has made good my promise to you. Wherever you turn your eyes, you see the trees loaded with fine fruit, many of them indeed breaking down, while the ground is covered with mellow apples, more than you could ever eat, my son, in all your life time."

George looked in silence on the wide wilderness of fruit; he marked the busy humming bees, and heard the gay notes of birds; then lifting his eyes, filled with shining moisture, he said, softly, to his father, "Well, Pa, only forgive me this time, and see if I ever be so stingy any more."

When George was about six years old, he was made the wealthy master of a hatchet! of which, like most boys, he was immoderately fond, and was constantly going about, chopping every thing that came in his way.

One day in the garden, where he had often amused himself hacking his mother's pea-bushes, he unluckily tried the edge of his hatchet on the body of a beautiful young English cherry tree, which he barked so terribly, that I don't believe the tree ever got the better of it.

The next morning, the old gentleman, finding out what had befallen his favourite tree, came into the house, and asked for the author of the mischief, declaring at the same time, that he would not have taken five guineas for the tree.

Nobody could tell him any thing about it. Presently George and his little hatchet made their appearance. "George," said his father, "do you know who killed that beautiful little cherry tree yonder in the garden?"

This was a tough question; and George staggered under it for a moment; but quickly recovered himself; and looking at his father, with the sweet face of youth, brightened with the charm of honesty, he bravely cried out, "I can't tell a lie, Pa; you know I can't tell a lie. I did it with my little hatchet."

"Run to my arms, my dearest boy," said his father; "you have paid me for my tree a thousand times; and I hope my son will always be hero enough to tell the truth, let come what will come."

LANGUAGE.

Language is human speech, or a set of articulate sounds, used by any nation or people to convey their ideas to each other.

Grammar is the art of speaking and writing any language with propriety.

Orthography is that part of grammar, which teaches the nature and power of letters, and the just method of spelling words.

A *letter* is the first principle, or least part of a word.

The letters of a language are called the *alphabet*, which in the English language are *twenty-six* in number.

Letters are divided into vowels and consonants.

A *vowel* is a letter, which can be perfectly sounded by itself; or without moving the parts of the mouth.

A *consonant* is a letter, which cannot be perfectly sounded by itself; but, joined with a vowel, forms an articulate or significant sound.

The vowels are *a, e, i, o, u,* and sometimes, *w* and *y*.

W and *y* are consonants, when they begin a word or syllable; but in every other situation they are called vowels.

A *diphthong* is the union of *two* vowels in one syllable; as *ea* in *beat*, *ou* in *sound*.

A *triphthong* is the union of *three* vowels in one syllable; as; *ieu* in *adieu; lieu*.

A *syllable* is a sound, either simple or compounded, pronounced by a single impulse or effort of the voice, and constituting a word or part of a word: as *man, man-ful*.

Words are articulate, or significant sounds, which are used to express our ideas.

A word of *one* syllable is called   a *mon'osyllable,*
A word of *two* syllables,   a *dis'syllable,*
A word of *three* syllables,   a *tris'yllable;*
A word of *four* or more syllables,   a *pol'ysyllable.*

56457 370.974
B95

Date Due

APR 1 7 1990			
279			

NYACK MISSIONARY COLLEGE
NYACK, NEW YORK